Secrets FOR WINNING AT WORK

20 Inspirational Keys For Success In Your Job & Career

By Mike Murdock

Tulsa, Oklahoma

Secrets for Winning at Work —
20 Inspirational Keys for Success in Your Job and Career
ISBN 1-56292-048-0
Copyright © 1993 by Mike Murdock

Published by Honor Books
P.O. Box 55388
Tulsa, Oklahoma 74155-1388

CONTENTS

- SAM WALTON — Wal-Mart

- MARY KAY ASH — Mary Kay Cosmetics

- S. TRUETT CATHY — Chick-Fil-A, Inc.

- DAVE THOMAS — Wendy's International

- WALT DISNEY — Walt Disney Productions

- RAY KROC — McDonald's

INTRODUCTION

Most of our adult lives are spent working. Taking into account commuting time, overtime, thinking about our jobs, and worrying over work, we spend more of our waking hours in the office, at the factory, on the road, behind the desk than we do at home.

But too many of us find our jobs dull, laborious, and repetitive, an irritating necessity of life, like death and taxes. How many people have said, "I like the work but hate my job," or "How can I like my work? It's just a job," or "The only joy I get at work is when the little hand on the clock says it's five o'clock."

This is a reality shared by countless workers, but the above remarks were made by a high-ranking corporate executive. His salary is in the six figures, he keeps three secretaries busy, and oversees the work of five hundred employees from behind his great mahogany desk. You may envy his job. You might think, "Nice work, if you can get it." Yet this executive finds his work taxing, stressfully repetitive, and tedious. Whatever initial enthusiasm he had to achieve his early goals, along the way he lost it.

It's true for so many of us. Whether blue collar, pink collar, or white collar, workers across the country feel frustrated and unsatisfied on the job.

Jim Mitchell, a television journalist in Louisville, Kentucky, hit the nail on the head: "Too many workers would rather get home than get ahead."

The media have picked up on America's lack of enthusiasm for working, citing problems of poor quality, reduced productivity, and declining services. In an attempt to find some answers, management experts have turned outside of our own country and culture. They come back with the exemplar of the Japanese worker, happy, healthy, better motivated, devoted to the company job. But the rigid conformity and dronelike discipline is ultimately counterproductive to innovation and progress. Put more succinctly, it's just not the American way of doing things.

So, as we began writing this book, we had to ask ourselves this question: Is it possible to combine *excellence* — quality, productivity, service — with *enjoyment?*

We firmly believe the answer is:

YES! Every American has the right and the ability to find fulfillment in their work. What we have forgotten is that *the key to personal progress, profit, and productivity is enjoyment!*

Whether you are a business manager, secretary, computer programmer, sales representative, engineer, office manager, factory worker, actor, athlete, teacher, or homemaker, we hope that you'll find on each page insights and attitudes that can lead you to find joy in the work you do.

Mark Twain once wrote, "The higher the pay in enjoyment the worker gets out of [his labors], the higher shall be his pay in money also."

"The highest reward for a man's toil is not what he gets for it, but what he becomes by it."

Ruskin

Chapter 1

LIVE WITH BALANCE

It was Monday, six o'clock in the evening, time for supper (or dinner — whatever you call the evening meal at your house). The four-year-old stared at the rather full plate of lasagna in front of him. He liked lasagna, and from past experience, he knew this was going to be good lasagna.

He looked at his full plate and then at the serving dish. There was a lot of lasagna in that serving dish — enough to last two adults and a four-year-old for several meals. We're talking lots of lasagna — good lasagna, and lots of it. Sounds wonderful to some of us.

The four-year-old's mother had been busy for several days, getting ready to teach a summer children's program. Thus, this meal was the second in a row at which she had served lasagna. Remember, it was good lasagna, yes, but still, it was, again, lasagna. And there was a *lot* of lasagna.

The four-year-old looked at his full plate of lasagna and then surveyed the still-almost-full serving dish of lasagna. He calculated the situation. Good lasagna, and a lot of good lasagna, yes. But the perceptive four-year-old seemed to behold a week of lasagna staring him in the face that Monday evening. With quiet firmness, he announced to his mom that Monday evening, "I'll eat this lasagna today and tomorrow. But I'm not eating it next Friday."

Maybe you know how he felt. Even though lasagna might be your favorite food, you probably don't want to eat lasagna — or whatever your favorite food is, even prime rib, fried chicken or lobster — every meal, day in and day out.

We crave variety, not sameness. Most of us want some degree of variety in the activities of our lives. Sleeping may be a favorite activity of yours, but it's unlikely you want to sleep twenty-four hours a day. The same thought holds for any of the activities in which we might engage. However much we enjoy *any* activity, we wouldn't want to do it *all* the time, every hour and minute of every day.

The point is this: balance is important in all of life, not just in the foods we choose. Achieving balance is certainly important in being happy in the job you sometimes can't stand.

More than a few folks have put all their eggs of happiness in one basket — their work. Perhaps the cultural conditioning of men leaves them especially vulnerable to this problem. Women, however, are gaining on men in this area. This over-investment in work by women and men is questionable progress. Just as we wouldn't be happy eating lasagna every meal (even *great* lasagna), we will hinder our happiness in our jobs if all we do is work. Expecting your job alone to provide fullness of satisfaction in life is a mistake.

People come nearer to enjoying their work when they engage in other activities besides work. Like what? Like rest and play and family and other people and hobbies. Like helping others and worshiping and learning and taking walks and looking at the clouds and the flowers. Like occasionally doing absolutely nothing.

One thing I enjoy about the seashore is the rhythmic motion of the waves rolling in and then receding. The waves roll in, and then they slide out. There's a balanced, rhythmic pattern to it all. What if the waves only rolled in and never slid out? It just wouldn't be the same, to say the least.

As with the waves, there's a time to go to work and a time to leave work behind for other pursuits. Failing to participate in this balanced rhythm of life may lead eventually to a measure of unhappiness even in a job you may love, not to mention the job you sometimes can't stand.

If just about all you are doing is working, no wonder you are not as happy in your work as you would like to be. It's time to take a fresh look at your priorities in life — not just in your job.

"In order to succeed,
you must know
what you are doing,
like what you are doing,
and believe in what
you are doing."

Will Rogers

Chapter 2

TWENTY KEYS FOR SUCCESS IN YOUR JOB AND CAREER

KEY #1

ACCEPT WORK AS GOD'S GIFT, NOT AS PUNISHMENT

...to rejoice in his labour; this is the gift of God.
Ecclesiastes 5:19

The first — and most important — key to winning at work is to rejoice in your labor, to find fulfillment in what you have been called to do, to derive satisfaction from your work.

Millions wake up each morning. . .dreading the day. Sarcasm, screaming, and conversations crammed with worry fill up the kitchens, bedrooms and homes throughout our nation every morning. In fact, many times what is perceived as a marriage or family problem is actually a career or work problem. That is why discovering what God intends for you to do with your life is the basis for the full apprehension of His gift of work.

It is amazing how many people spend forty hours a week at a job for which they are totally unsuited. Statistics tell us that seventy percent of the labor force is working on the wrong job, which means that they have gifts and talents that are not being fully or properly utilized. That's why they end up frustrated and miserable.

However, thousands of people are beginning to wake up to the fact that a job and career can be the most exciting part of their life. In fact, if you have chosen the right kind of work for your personality and calling, it will be the source of great delight for your entire lifetime.

Most important, when you treat your work as a gift from the Lord, you become a problem solver in today's broken world — a light shining in the darkness.

Such work is a gift from God in three powerful ways. First, it is a gift to you personally. It helps you discover and use dormant qualities. It exposes you to other people, forcing you to learn the art of communication — speaking with and listening to others.

Worthy work forces you to think outside yourself, provides a focus for your energy, and destroys self-absorption.

Second, your work is a gift from God for others around you. What you do contributes to something beyond yourself. You may be only one step in a complex process but without you and what you contribute, the process would be incomplete. When you do your part and more, those around you see your contribution and are inspired to live up to the standard that you set. Your work then becomes a gift to the world around you. It creates life, movement, progress, energy.

Third, your work is a gift of God to your family. The way you work becomes the example they will follow. Therefore, through your diligence in your job, your family is led to be equally diligent in what they do. Of course, your job also provides the financial means through which you take care of your family's needs. As your financial resources expand, you are able to provide gifts that express your love and care for them, going beyond just meeting their basic needs for shelter, food, clothing.

Without your job, everything important to you would be jeopardized.

I feel that the people who work on my staff are the most efficient, effective group of co-laborers I have ever been associated with in my life. God has given me fabulous, beautiful, dedicated, thinking people to help me in my ministry. I find them absolutely remarkable. One reason they are so incredible is because they have learned to accept work as God's gift and not as punishment.

I have worked to make my ministry one in which people can release their God-given gifts and talents. When someone on my staff becomes unhappy, I can sense it. How do you recognize an unhappy employee? One way is by his productivity. When a worker is not productive, it is because he is dissatisfied or unfulfilled. If a person is not excited about his work, it shows up not only in his attitude and behavior, but also in his output.

When one of my co-workers shows signs of being unhappy or begins to fall behind in his productivity, I will call him aside and ask him, "Is anything wrong? Is there a problem at home? Are you having troubles with your finances?" I don't want an unhappy employee on my payroll because a disgruntled worker will cause problems and destroy the morale and productivity of others.

That's why we see entire companies and industries go millions of dollars in debt and end up in bankruptcy. It doesn't take long to suffer a major loss if your organization has unhappy or dissatisfied employees.

Because I take my own work so seriously, I believe that when someone in my ministry is unhappy it is my fault. More likely than not, I have tried to place that individual in a position of responsibility he is not ready, qualified, or suited to fulfill. Sometimes I become interested in a person and will say to him, "I am so impressed by you that I would like for you to take on this job. Will you do it for me?" And, of course, out of sheer loyalty that individual will get involved in that project and try to carry it out even though he may be incapable of handling it. He usually ends up overworked and underproductive. I placed him on the wrong task.

Another indication that a person is unhappy on the job is carelessness. As a general rule, people are careful about what they are interested in. Carelessness is almost always the result of a lack of enthusiasm. When I see an individual who is continuously careless, I know he has lost interest in his work and needs to be moved to a more challenging position. I must either find him a different function in my ministry, or find him a different ministry in which to function. One way or the other, he is in the wrong place.

When people are constantly asking for time off, continually looking forward to vacations, always needing leisure time, it is a sign that they are working on the wrong job.

It is human nature to pursue what brings enjoyment and avoid that which does not. If you enjoy your work, then you won't be constantly trying to get away from it.

I know a man named Morris Plotts who is almost eighty years old. For many, many years he has labored diligently and tirelessly in churches all over East Africa. I have spent months and months with him there on the mission field. He loves what he is doing. He is not looking for time off or a way out, because he enjoys his work.

If you love what you're doing, then you don't want to quit. If you want to quit, then you don't love your work. It's just that simple.

Work is not punishment; it is God's gift to His children. It is designed not only to provide for their material needs, but also to bring them enjoyment, satisfaction, and fulfillment in life.

"Don't just make a living; design a life."

Jim Rohn

KEY #2
RECOGNIZE GOD AS YOUR TRUE EMPLOYER AND CELEBRATE YOUR BOSS
With good will doing service, as to the Lord, and not to men.
Ephesians 6:7

As a minister of the Lord, I tell my staff, "I am not your boss, God is. What you do, do as unto the Lord."

That may sound a bit trite, something of a religious cliche, but it is true nevertheless.

You would be amazed at the number of employees who get angry at their employer because they feel that he doesn't pay them enough or treats them in ways they consider unfair. This is the cause of much job dissatisfaction and employer-employee friction, distrust, and animosity.

But when God is your authority, you look to Him regarding your working conditions. When you learn to view God, not man, as your true employer — as your source of wisdom, knowledge, and provision — then you begin to see things in the proper perspective. You no longer expect man to provide what only your heavenly Father can supply. You look for your sense of appreciation, job satisfaction, and reward not from your earthly boss but from your true Employer.

With God as your true employer, you are free to be the servant of your earthly employer. As Christ said, . . .**Whosoever will be chief among you, let him be your servant** (Matt. 20:27).

17

You can recognize that your boss is not perfect. The stresses and pressures he feels may make him erratic, unpredictable and difficult. However, he is the channel through which God has chosen to use and bless you. You can celebrate this person in specific and powerful ways.

When I say, "celebrate your boss," I'm not talking about syrupy, cheap flattery or words and actions designed to manipulate.

Rather, I am talking about fully grasping the significance and value of those in authority around you. There is a reason they are in that specific position. Usually, it is because of personal dedication to excellence, the ability to be self-motivated and maintain focus when others are easily distracted.

Most people in authority:

■ Feel something others do not feel.

■ Know something others do not know.

■ Have explored territories others have not yet explored.

■ Handle stress more effectively than others.

Listen to those in authority. Observe their personal priorities. Focus on what they are focusing on.

How do you celebrate a boss?

1) Hear his instruction. When he speaks, give total and absolute focus. Listen thoroughly. Listen to what he *does not say.* Discern what your boss considers excellent performance. Learn him. Feel his heartbeat. Anticipate the direction his mind is going.

What does he notice with favor? What displeases him? What upsets or angers him? What creates joy on his countenance?

2) Repeat it. A person's mind can be on one thing while his mouth speaks another. It happens all the time. Countless times over the years, one of my staff has repeated something back to me and I discovered that I had spoken something in error...a day, date, color, name, place. Seek clarity, clarity, clarity. Repeating instructions assures you and your boss that you are heading in the right direction.

3) Write it. Always keep paper and pen in your hand when talking with your boss. "Faintest line is better than strongest mind." Memory can be fatally flawed. You can leave one discussion and get involved in another, quickly distracted. When you write down key points, you are free to pursue other things, coming back to the written instructions at any time, assured that you will still be on track.

Keep all instructions in one notebook. This helps you avoid a collection of half-notes, scribbled hurriedly. It reveals your commitment to an ordered way of doing things. Further, it reveals the value you place on the instruction. When your boss sees your notebook of instructions, it conveys that what he says actually matters to you. This is a catalyst for several things:

a) He will become increasingly more careful about what he says because he knows you are going to write it down.

b) Your words will become more important to him.

c) Knowing you are documenting encourages him toward accuracy and thoroughness in his instructions.

4) Do it. Do what you are instructed. Thoroughly. Immediately. Diligently. Everything you do sends a message. A signal. An impression. A photograph of your excellence.

5) Report it. Update your boss continually. Keep the memo or message short, concise, relevant. Avoid unnecessary data that distracts, lengthy recitations of problems.

6) Become your boss's number one problem-solver. Your worth to your boss is determined by the problems you solve for him. You will only be remembered for two things:

■ The problems you solve.

■ The problems you create.

Follow this advice adapted from Leon Uris in *The Executive Desk Book,* published by Van Nostrand Reinhold Company.

■ Is there a solution to this problem?

■ Say it or write it down.

■ Define it positively.

■ Have you forgotten anything.

■ Get additional information.

■ Look for more than one solution.

■ Welcome new ideas from others.

■ Check your solution and check yourself.

■ Don't look for one perfect solution. Rather aim for the best you can get under the circumstances or in your specific situation. Adapt!

■ Test your ego. Do you insist on being right? Or, are you looking for the right solution! There is a difference.

7) Ask him to help you improve. Be entirely open to every suggestion he makes to you about your performance. **Poverty and shame shall be to him that refuseth instruction: but he that regardeth reproof shall be honored** (Prov. 13:18).

8) Avoid the reputation of "complainer" at all costs. Never voice a negative without a reasonable and positive recommendation or alternative.

Never complain about what you permit. If something is bothering you, gently but firmly deal with it immediately. Do not let it build momentum.

"If you love your work, you'll be out there every day trying to do it the best you possibly can, and pretty soon everybody around will catch the passion from you — like a fever."

Sam Walton

KEY #3
PURSUE WORK COMPATIBLE WITH YOUR ABILITIES AND INTERESTS
Neglect not the gift that is in thee....
1 Timothy 4:14

The Apostle Paul encouraged his young disciple, Timothy, not to neglect his God-given abilities and interests. And wise Solomon in the Old Testament recognized particular and individual talents among people as evidenced in 2 Chronicles 2:7-14 where he called for various skilled workmen to supervise and carry out the work of constructing the temple of the Lord.

What you love deeply is a clue to the gifts you contain. What you hate is a clue to something you were created to alter or change. What saddens you is a clue to something you were created to heal or solve.

People are usually good at what they like to do. Yet, often we will hear someone say, "I love to do one thing, but God has called me to do something else."

Often that kind of attitude comes from our religious upbringing. I remember being taught that if God called me to go to Africa as a missionary, and I didn't want to go, then He would force me to do His will or else punish me with lifelong unhappiness if I didn't.

That is a very intriguing philosophy, isn't it? I was even afraid to go to the altar of the Lord and surrender my life to Him for fear that He would call me to do something I hated or for which I was totally unsuited and unqualified.

Can you imagine any father — especially our loving heavenly Father — thinking of ways to make His children miserable and unhappy? That is not the way our divine Creator operates. Instead, He links our purpose with our pleasure.

Now it is true that the divine link between what we love to do and what we are called to do is not always immediately obvious. That's why so many people are confused about what they are gifted to do and what they are called to do. Some seem to think that just because they have a talent for music, they must necessarily be obligated to devote their lives to the music ministry. That is not always the case. Generally, God calls us to what we love to do, what He has already given us the desire as well as the ability to do.

We must remember that the One Who created us knows how to give us the greatest satisfaction and pleasure. According to James 1:17 every good and every perfect gift comes down from God. The Bible also teaches that the Lord enjoys pleasuring His people. (Ps. 149:4.)

Pause for a moment and think of what you would like most to do with your life. To help you organize your thoughts, let me give you a little quick quiz:

1. What do you like to talk about most? If you are like the majority of people, you tend to talk about three topics: a) the things you hate, b) the things you love, and c) the things you fear. Be particularly conscious for several days of the kinds of conversations you have. Listen to yourself. Focus. Then, make a written list of what you have found yourself discussing.

2. What books do you like to read? What magazines do you

subscribe to? What types of movies and television programs do you enjoy most? Write them down.

3. If you could do anything in the world, knowing that it could not possibly fail, what would you choose to do? What would you tell God you wanted to do if you knew that you would be absolutely assured of succeeding? Write that down.

4. If you knew that God had granted you your request, what would you attempt to do *today* with your life? Write that down also.

5. What do you want others to say about your life when you have gone on to meet the Lord? Think of this as your own eulogy. Write it down.

These observations should give you a pretty good idea of what you like to do, what you want to do, what your purpose is and where you should begin in order to see your desire and personal mission come true.

Don't be discouraged if your interests seem to exceed your talents at this point. Don't be disheartened if your beginning steps seem small. Remember, your abilities are given to you in seed form. God doesn't create people complete because He knows that man's greatest pleasure comes from a sense of progress.

If you are making a thousand dollars a week right now, but think that you would be perfectly happy if you could only become a millionaire, you are no doubt right. You probably would be happy with a million dollars — for about three months. By that time you would be wanting to know how to invest your one million in order to double it to two million. Why? Because you are made to proceed and progress. As God's creation , you are pre-programmed for growth.

Like every living creature , man has an innate need to grow and expand. That's why God gives us seeds instead of plants, acorns instead of oak trees, babies instead of adults.

Parents love to see their children grow, learn and develop. In the same way, the whole point of our creation as the children of God is for a sense of progress. That's why you need to realize that your abilities come in seed form. What you are today is not what you will be a year from now, or ten years from now, or twenty years from now.

Even God Himself has a need to experience progress. He doesn't grow in knowledge, because all knowledge is His. He doesn't grow in wealth, because all the silver and all the gold are His. He doesn't grow in power, because all power is His. How does God grow? How does the Creator of the universe derive pleasure in progression?

If you and I are made in the image of God and have a need to grow, then God must have a need to grow. How does our heavenly Father grow? He grows by seeing His nature duplicated in us. God expands Himself through the nature of people. That's why the Bible speaks of our being partakers of His divine nature. (2 Pet. 1:4.)

That's one of the reasons I believe giving fascinates and pleases God. When He sees a person who gives, He sees His nature in that individual. God experiences pleasure through the extension and expansion of His own nature in others.

Once you realize that God gives you abilities in seed form, it is up to you to water, nurture, fertilize and grow that seed. The most important thing in life is not the fact that you have a purpose, but the fact that you know what that purpose is. You've got to know the purpose for which you were created. Once you do, you will choose work that is a challenge rather than work that is merely convenient.

I once met a man who had worked for the same company for twenty-seven years.

"You must really love your job," I said to him.

"No, as a matter of fact, I hate it," he confided in me.

"Then, why have you worked here all these years?" I asked.

"Because it's so convenient," he answered. "It's just ten minutes from my house."

Isn't it amazing that a man would endure torture for twenty-seven years just for the sake of personal convenience? Yet many people spend their lives at jobs they detest. They are simply awaiting retirement, a monthly pension and a gold watch. Such people never graduate to realize that their own accomplishments generate personal pleasure far greater than awards and blessings far more lasting than speeches.

If you are to win at work, you must discover what you are good at, get into it, and then stick to it. In this way, you can be fascinated and intrigued every day by what you are doing.

Someone has said, "Find something you love to do and you'll never have to work another day in your life."

"Every job is a self-portrait of the person who did it."

Zig Ziglar

KEY #4
LEARN EVERYTHING POSSIBLE ABOUT YOUR JOB
A wise man will hear; and will increase learning....
Proverbs 1:5

These sage words from Solomon are repeated in the New Testament by the Apostle Paul who wrote to young Timothy: ...**give attendance to reading.** ...(1 Tim. 4:13), and ...**Study to shew thyself approved unto God, a workman that needeth not to be ashamed...** (2 Tim. 2:15).

Hosea proclaimed, **My people are destroyed for lack of knowledge** (Hos. 4:6). It is interesting that Hosea does not say that *Satan* could destroy you. . .he says that *ignorance* could destroy you.

Ignorance is deadly.

Knowledge is the only bridge you and I have to walk across the vast chasm of ignorance. The right information will not only promote us, it will even motivate us. It will reposition us to receive God's greatest blessing in our lives.

Proverbs 11:9 says, . . .**through knowledge shall the just be delivered.**

Some people think that if they know God then they have all the knowledge they need. No, it is possible to be right and not bright, to have a clean heart and an empty head. That is true, believe me, because I have met such people all over this country.

29

God does not do a mind transplant at the time of conversion. Receiving God into your life means that you have access to proper information. It does not mean that such information has automatically been transferred into your mind or implemented into your life. That is something you must do for yourself.

Remember, an experience with God is instantaneous, but the expertise of God is progressive. Your heart can be changed by salvation, but your circumstances are changed by wisdom. That's why you can create your own world through the laws of God.

There is a difference between the life of God and the laws of God, between the King and the Kingdom, just as there is a difference between the salvation of God and the wisdom of God.

Just as Godly knowledge and wisdom are necessary for success in the spiritual realm, so earthly knowledge and wisdom are necessary for success in the natural realm. That's why you need to learn everything possible about your job.

Just as importantly, you have to learn *continuously*. Remember that you cannot create a different future with the same information. So you must seek out new and additional information all the time. Read magazines, go to seminars, frequent the library and bookstores.

Keep in mind that it is not enough to have accurate information, you must also have full information. Let me give you an example.

Accurate information is that a person who rebels against God is going to hell. But full information is that repentance will alter that situation.

Consequently, the successful person makes sure he has full *and* accurate information. The only full and accurate information that ever comes to us is that which we pursue purposely. That's why Solomon wrote that if a person wants wisdom, he must *seek* it.

Someone has said that the distance between success and mediocrity is due to three forces:

1. *Information.* The successful person knows something that others have not yet discovered or cared to pursue.

2. *Motivation.* The successful person's projects are more defined and compelling. They grab attention and clearly convey the motivation and enthusiasm of the individual.

3. *Associations.* The successful person knows how to be a bridge instead of a barrier between people, a door instead of a wall. Further, the successful person knows that success may be simply a one-word university: respect. Respect for people and their time, opinions, memories, fears, goals, wounds.

If you want to win at work, accumulate and digest every bit of information available about your job. Knowledge is power, influence, money. Knowledge is worth everything it may cost you to obtain it. That's why Solomon wrote: **Wisdom is the principal thing; therefore get wisdom: and with all thy getting get understanding** (Prov. 4:7).

"Waste your money and you're only out of money, but waste your time and you've lost a part of your life."

Dr. Michael LeBoeuf

KEY #5
DON'T BE A TIME THIEF

Let him that stole steal no more: but rather let him labour, working with his hands the thing which is good, that he may have to give to him that needeth.

Redeeming the time, because the days are evil.
Ephesians 4:28; 5:16

I love to quote this passage to an employee who is stealing time.

How does a person steal time from his employer? By coming in at eight-thirty instead of eight o'clock. By spending the first twenty minutes of the day getting coffee and reading the morning paper. By dilly-dallying during office hours. By making unnecessary trips to the water cooler or rest room. By chatting with co-workers instead of attending to business. By making lengthy personal phone calls or running personal errands on company time. By stretching coffee breaks. By leaving early for lunch. By coming back late from lunch. By "knocking off" early in the afternoon.

How do you steal time from yourself and others? You steal time when you don't have a planned schedule for your day or your life, when you have no specified time frame in which to accomplish specific tasks. You steal time from yourself and others when you procrastinate, when you put off dealing with issues and projects that need to be faced and handled right away.

Benjamin Franklin once said, "Dost thou love life? Then do not squander time, for that is the stuff life is made of."

People who waste time, waste their very lives.

When I waste time, I become very frustrated. There is an unconscious irritation that bothers me. I feel bad about what I am doing and about myself as well.

But when I make up lost time, when I make time count for me instead of against me, when I redeem the time, then I feel more responsible, more productive, more enthusiastic. I also have more self-respect and a more positive outlook.

So will you. Others will think more highly of you, too. If you truly want to win at work, don't waste time. Rather redeem the time, because the days are not only evil, they are short.

"The secret of your future is hidden in your daily routine."

Mike Murdock

KEY #6
KEEP A DAILY TO-DO LIST AND ESTABLISH DEADLINES
To every thing there is a season, and a time to every purpose under the heaven.
Ecclesiastes 3:1

The Apostle Paul wrote in Philippians 3:13, **This one thing I do....** That is a good rule for you to follow as well. Create a written plan, set priorities and fix a time frame in which to accomplish each item in your plan. Otherwise you run the risk of being swept away with trivia. For example, did you know that the average American sees or hears 560 advertisements in a single day? Without written priorities, the "messiness" of daily living will continuously distract us and defeat our pursuits.

Here are six pointers for making daily scheduling a useful habit:

1) Review thoroughly your responsibilities.

2) Determine the priorities that will bring the greatest benefit to you, your boss and your company.

3) Create routines for the things you must do every week or every day. For example, if you have a staff meeting, do it the same time every week; if you have your hair cut monthly, schedule it for the same day and time.

4) Delegate wisely but never dump. This requires you to know specifically what your own abilities are as well as those of

the people around you. You can then make sure that every person is prepared and ready to assume responsibility for what must be accomplished.

5) Schedule solitude. Confer with yourself. Successful people know the value of using solitude to put pieces of a problem together. . .to do what some call "super thinking." Your opinion matters but you must get alone to discover what it really is.

6) Know ahead of time the purpose and desired end of all appointments. Never schedule an open-ended appointment. Make it a habit to state the starting time and the ending time. Remember that you cannot save time — you can only spend it and successful people know how to spend it wisely.

John F. Kennedy was known as a man on the move. Whatever he was doing, wherever he was going, he always seemed to be in haste toward something else. He never gave the appearance of having time to spare. He was constantly en route, in action, on the move, giving necessary time to people and projects, but continually on his way to the next priority.

I think that kind of "plan-ahead" attitude and behavior has to be cultivated.

I once read that Mary Kay Ash, founder of Mary Kay Cosmetics , said that she had learned to write down each morning six things she was going to accomplish that day. Not ten. Ten was too many. If she only did eight of the things on her list, she felt that she had failed to accomplish as much as she should have. Not three. Because that was not enough to challenge her.

One of the secrets to her phenomenal success was that she had learned to keep a daily to-do list and to establish deadlines.

You don't have a goal unless you have a fixed time reference in which to reach it. In fact, someone has defined a goal as a dream with a deadline.

Of all the people I have known in my lifetime, Oral Roberts probably has more concentration than any three of four of the others. His sense of timing and focus is incredible. Once he has set his mind on something, he cannot be moved one iota from it until it has been resolved to his satisfaction.

One time he and I were working on a musical composition in which he felt impressed to include three phrases. One was "don't give up your dream." Another was "don't turn loose of your vision." The third was "it's not over yet." And to be quite honest, "yet" is not an easy word to find a rhyme for. The only word I could think of was "bet," and I was not at all sure that was appropriate.

I also tried to tell Brother Roberts that "don't turn loose of your dream" is not very "singable." But he insisted on including it because he said he was sure that it was supposed to be there with the others. We kept working with that song until we found the right combination of words to express what Brother Roberts knew in his heart to be the message of the Lord for the hour.

The reason we were successful is because he refused to give up until he had accomplished what he had set out to do. Every time I worked with Brother Roberts and his staff I was impressed by the fact that everything worked by a deadline, a specific time frame in which a certain job was to be completed.

My staff can tell you that I work by schedules and deadlines. When they tell me that they will have a certain project completed by next week, I ask, "What day next week?" When they tell me the day, I ask, "What time that day?" I never give them a goal without establishing a specific time reference in which to achieve that goal.

If you learn to set priorities and deadlines, you will soon find that a fixed schedule is not a burden but an aid. It helps you to know where you are at all times and what you should do next. It soon becomes natural to live by a routine and a pre-determined plan.

Creativity can work even within the confines of deadlines; in fact, it can work even better that way.

When you set a goal to accomplish a specific amount of work within a specified time period, you set your creative process in motion. Setting a deadline unlocks something within you that will excite and motivate you to be more creative than you ever thought possible.

"Excellence is to do a common thing in an uncommon way."

Booker T. Washington

KEY #7
ASK FOR GOD'S WISDOM DURING DECISION-MAKING
If any of you lack wisdom, let him ask of God, that giveth to all men liberally, and upbraideth not; and it shall be given him.
James 1:5

Success depends almost totally on decisions.

Your decisions.

The quality and timeliness of your decisions.

Sam Walton, the late billionaire once said, "I never make decisions about investing in a company for where it will be eighteen months from now. I always ask myself where the company will actually be in ten years."

He thought long term.

That's how to determine the depth of wisdom you contain: How far ahead do you think? How far ahead do you plan? The wiser you are, the farther ahead you plan...and you make decisions based on long term rather than short term.

The drug addict has made a short-term decision — to feel good for a few seconds. The alcoholic has made a short term decision — to forget about his problems for a few hours. The adulteress has made a short term decision — to experience physical pleasure for an hour.

All losers have one common denominator and thread running through their lives. They make short-term decisions.

In other words, they make decisions that create an immediate desired result, while creating a possible risk that can sabotage their future.

Decision making is an emotional current and moment. Plus, today's society moves so fast, we rarely stop and think logically when confronted with most events requiring a decision. We just plow ahead, only realizing the consequences later, when the results of our decision begin to surface. In fact, many heartaches and tragedies in life can be traced to a bad decision. Consequently, successful people have found that major decisions should never be made during the following times:

a) When you are too hungry.

b) When you are too angry.

c) When you are too lonely.

d) When you are too tired.

e) When someone unsympathetic to your cause in life controls the deadline or outcome.

f) When you have not considered every consequence of your decision.

g) When you have not considered wise counsel of those qualified to advise you.

h) When you have not invested time in the presence of God.

Sometimes when I am facing a major decision in my life and I have no direction or course I feel comfortable with, I do a little mental exercise. In my mind, I picture sitting at a counseling table with several outstanding Bible characters — Abraham, David,

Solomon, the Apostle Paul, Moses, Joshua. Of course, Jesus Himself sits at the head of the table. Then I ask my "advisors" what their thoughts are on the decision I am facing.

Abraham advises me to be patient and give more time to permit God to work and move. Why? He almost destroyed his entire life by getting ahead of God and not giving God space to provide Isaac.

Solomon knew that the eyes of man are never satisfied and that there is not enough money on earth to keep man satiated. Thus, he advises me to "fear God and keep his commandments. This is the whole duty of man."

Moses advises me to stay closer to God than to people and to choose God's voice over man's. Obviously, he got too close to people and lost out on the triumph and victory of the land of Canaan.

I move around the table and hear the wisdom of the ages applied to my problem.

Finally, I come to Jesus. If I listen with my whole heart and honestly seek His wisdom, I know my decisions will be the right ones — those that will keep me on course and bring the most benefit to His cause.

However, too many times when facing a tough decision or a perplexing problem, we make a major mistake. We only "think" a prayer without expressing it orally. Worse, when we do express our desire, it is in the form of a wish rather than a request. We will say, "I wish I knew what to do," rather than saying, "Lord, tell me what to do."

The Bible says that if we need wisdom, we should ask God for it, and it will be given us. If you are facing a difficult decision, don't just wish for wisdom; ask the Lord for His divine wisdom. See Him sitting at the counsel table, waiting for you to approach Him, waiting to receive your request for His guidance, and ready to give you His undivided attention until you have heard His response.

Frankly, I have found that my most carefully laid plans often have fatal flaws that can only be revealed in the presence of God. So, get alone with the Lord and seek His heavenly counsel and advice. Often problems and decisions that have baffled us for hours or days can be cleared up in a matter of minutes by a word from the Lord.

Proverbs 16:33 says, **The lot is cast into the lap; but the whole disposing thereof is of the Lord.** The *New International Version* translates this verse: **The lot is cast into the lap, but its every decision is from the Lord.**

In John 16:13 Jesus told His disciples: **. . . when he, the Spirit of truth, is come, he will guide you into all truth. . . .** When faced with a crucial decision, don't go into a panic. Instead, stop, disconnect from everything around you, and go into neutral. Be still and listen for the voice of the Lord. You will be amazed at the wisdom that the Holy Spirit, the Divine Counselor, will impart to you.

"People are not driven into perfection by rules, but rather driven by example."

Fred Smith

KEY #8
USE CRITICISM TO YOUR ADVANTAGE

Poverty and shame shall be to him that refuseth instruction: but he that regardeth reproof shall be honoured.
Proverbs 13:18

I tell people who want to be successful to get on the positive side of criticism, to learn to take constructive criticism and make it work for them rather than against them. Such an attitude takes the sting out of correction, reproof, or even persecution.

You want to be the best employee your boss has ever had in his entire life. Who can train you better as to his criteria than the boss himself? So, constantly permit and invite his scrutiny. Believe me, you will definitely stand out from the crowd.

I dare you to go to your supervisor on a regular basis and ask if he sees ways you can improve your performance or make a better contribution. You will be amazed at the positive reaction you will get.

Teach yourself to approach your boss with an open heart to his criticism. Say, "I need to learn all I can from you in order to be an outstanding employee. I want to meet privately with you on a regular basis. During each session, I want you to criticize my work from every possible angle. I make a commitment to you that I will not be defensive about your criticism. I will listen carefully and do everything I can to incorporate your desires into my work. I also promise that I will make suggestions to you about improving the business."

Criticism also creates a crisis. And, crisis reveals. Crisis energizes. Crisis stimulates. Crisis makes you use your faith.

In fact, criticism and crisis mean you have got to change. Change reveals. Change energizes. Change stimulates. Change makes you use your faith.

Criticism and crisis create the opportunity for you to change:

- What you are doing
- What you are saying
- What you are listening to
- What you know

It's true, of course, that some things never change. Cockroaches, for example, have lived on the earth for 250 million years without changing in any way. However, who wants the cockroach as a role model?

Believe me, the way to defeat the negative effects of criticism is to get on the positive side of it. Invite it. Embrace the crisis and the opportunity for change that it offers. You will be absolutely amazed at how it will set you apart and mark you as the successful, confident, productive person God intends you to be.

"Try not to become a
man of success but rather
try to become a
man of value."

Albert Einstein

KEY #9
BE HONEST ABOUT YOUR MISTAKES
He that covereth his sins shall not prosper: but whoso confesseth and forsaketh them shall have mercy.
Proverbs 28:13

Mistakes happen.

Regardless of how much we want to be perfect, we are still simply human. Every day of our life, we make mistakes of some sort. Don't cover them up. Don't lie. Be bold. Be direct. Be approachable about them.

Almost every successful company or person has chalked up a list of mistakes or failures.

Look at 3M. Here's a multi-billion dollar company that makes over sixty thousand products. Did you know it grew out of a mistake? Originally, the company planned to make sandpaper. However, because of a worthless mineral, the company was forced to either go under or make significant changes. The owners could have thrown up their hands, blamed each other, grown resentful that their plans did not work out.

Instead, they said, "What have we learned from this mistake? How can we use our people and equipment differently?" They quickly admitted the failure of the first effort and turned their energy and intellect to making something positive happen as a result. Now, everyone agrees that 3M is one of the most successful and creative enterprises anywhere in the world today.

Or, consider Thomas Edison. He made ten thousand experiments before he developed the filament that would carry electric current and produce light. He made 9,999 mistakes. Yet, each one taught him what would not work and through the process of elimination, he discovered what would work. Edison was known to have said, "Success is ninety-nine percent perspiration and one percent inspiration."

Don't you know too many people who are defensive and immediately try to blame other people, circumstances or even God Himself for any problems that surface? It is the rare person who has the confidence to acknowledge his own mistakes and take action to correct his errors. Yet it is such a person who has the power to diffuse defensiveness, bitterness, hostility and resentment in others.

That's why admission is better than deceit or cover-up. A confession opens the way to mercy. When someone on my staff comes to me and confesses a fault or failing, I am much more inclined to show that individual compassion and forgiveness than if he tries to cover up his mistake or deny his error.

Here's how to go about admission and confession:

a) Once you know you have made a mistake, find an option for correction that will prevent losses to the company.

b) Talk to your boss immediately. State what happened, without excuses. Tell him what you will do about correcting the mistake and ask for his approval to proceed. Reassure your boss that you realize your mistake has cost the company money, perhaps caused him embarrassment, and made the team look bad. Tell him that you will do everything in your power to make sure the same mistake never happens again and outline at least two specific preventive steps you will take to prevent future similar failure.

c) Be willing to point out why you think the mistake happened. Perhaps you did not receive adequate information or felt you were required to give other projects more priority. Never, never, complain about or try to throw the blame on others. Don't become a "victim." However, if other people are involved, do not hesitate to explain the situation from your point of view.

Often, I walk through the different rooms of our office complex and feel things — attitudes, actions, even thoughts — all around me. I believe that mental and spiritual entities have a presence just as much as physical and material entities. I believe I can sense hostility, anger, resentment, fear, animosity, insecurity, and other emotions.

But my special sensory perception is not limited to mental or spiritual activity.

I remember one time when I entered my office and immediately sensed that something was wrong. I walked straight to a filing cabinet, opened it, and lifted up a file. There, I discovered a stack of month-old checks that the secretary had never deposited.

She looked at me and said, "I forgot all about those checks. How did you know they were there?"

It wasn't because I am incredibly brilliant, but because I am incredibly sensitive. It was not something I figured out in my head but something I sensed in my spirit.

I do that kind of thing quite often. I will sense that something is wrong, that things are not right for some reason. Sometimes I will get this feeling when I am a thousand miles from home and will call back to see what is happening. That is my calling, my burden, as well as my spiritual gift.

But on the other hand, such knowing without seeing is not limited to those in the ministry. I truly believe that many times an employer has the same capacity to sense when things are not quite right. He can feel when someone is being dishonest. When this is the case, the employee who has made mistakes and admits them immediately gains the respect of the employer or supervisor.

There have been times when an employee's mistake has cost me a great deal of time, energy, or money. But when that person came to me in earnest confession and contrition, I could not find it in my heart to chastise him. He looked so hurt and crushed already that the last thing I wanted to do was to add insult to injury. Instead, I was moved to show kindness and mercy.

On the other hand, if I find that someone is sneaking around behind my back or constantly blaming problems on other people, then I have a tendency to become the interrogator and the inquisitor. I find myself wanting to expose the person who is being deceitful.

The same is true with any good employer.

An employee, honest about his mistakes, always has an advantage in the long-run, even if acknowledgement of the error causes personal pain or momentary embarrassment.

You will never be truly successful in work or in life until you learn to be honest about your mistakes — honest with yourself and honest with others.

As someone said, "Honesty is not the best policy; it is the only policy."

"In a career you either go
forward or backward;
you don't stand still.
Every manager must
continually improve his or her
skills in a lifetime
self-improvement program."

Mary Kay Ash

KEY #10
BE QUICK TO ASK FOR HELP AND INFORMATION WHEN NEEDED

A wise man is strong; yea, a man of knowledge increaseth strength.

For by wise counsel thou shalt make thy war: and in a multitude of counselors there is safety.

Proverbs 24:5,6

Here are five ways to ask for help and get it:

1) Select the right person to ask. This means that every time you meet someone, you must be a diligent listener and observer. Realize that there are people everywhere who take genuine pleasure in sharing what they know or have seen with others. However, it is up to you to find those people and build a relationship that will make them approachable.

2) Select the right time to ask. Don't approach another person when they are obviously rushed, anxious or stressed. Be courteous and arrange in advance for a moment of their time and counsel.

3) Select the right questions to ask. When you approach a respected person with one or two specific questions, you demonstrate that you have sought them because you believe their talent will have a *specific* impact on your need or problem. You show respect for their expertise and willingness to help you. You demonstrate that you have given serious thought to incorporating what they say to you into your own work. They will know they are not wasting their time with you.

4) Give them credit for their advice and counsel. When the person you have approached for help sees you using what they have recommended, you build them up. You demonstrate that they have invested their talents in you wisely.

5) Express your thanks specifically. Tell the person exactly how their advice and counsel helped you improve, change or grow. Sure, "thanks" is good, "Thanks for helping me understand that my real problem was time-management" is even better.

Remember that someone who is capable of greatly blessing you is always observing you.

I believe it is a form of pride to avoid asking for help. When we have too much pride, we will not admit that we need outside help and information. Just as importantly, we rob the gifted people around us of the blessing of reaching out to us and imparting the wisdom and knowledge they have about some specific problem or need.

Another aspect of asking for help lies within the art of delegation. When you are in a position to do it, delegation can be one of your most effective leadership and teaching tools. When you are effective as a delegator, you convey your respect for others, your openness to their help, and your humility. After all, no person can know or do everything. No individual has the talent to accomplish every function in a business.

Consequently, most successful people are delegators.

Here are six important steps to successful delegation:

1) Pinpoint the task. When you are able to specify exactly what you want done, you reduce the possibility for error, lost time, misunderstanding.

2) Select the right person. This requires that you know the people who work for you. You must know their strengths, interests, capabilities. You must know their limitations, as well. Otherwise, you will throw people into situations for which they are not prepared. When they fail, it is a reflection on you, as well.

3) Make the assignment clear. When to start, when to finish, who else to involve, the outcome expected. This means you have to think these things through in advance. Successful delegators know that delegation is not dumping!

4) Supply support or additional help as necessary. Let the person you are delegating to know what resources to call on in order to get the job done. Open up educational opportunities; make time for interim discussions and check points.

5) Check on progress. Don't expect the other person to initiate discussions. Approach him. Ask for specific feedback. Remove barriers that impede progress.

6) Evaluate and reward. Too many tasks get delegated and once completed, the individual behind any successes feels as if he has been tossed into a "black hole." Be on the lookout for ways to acknowledge successful completion of a delegated task. This is another situation where a simple "thanks" is good. However, a more specific statement such as, "Thanks, you did a great job on the layout for the new magazine article and you did it in record time" is even better!

When you are the person being delegated to, you can use

these same steps to assure that you accomplish what has been asked of you. Upon receiving the instructions or delegated task, ask your boss, "Let me see if I understand everything. You want me to _____ (the task) because you believe my experience in _____ (capability) is appropriate. I will start by _____ and complete the assignment by _____. I will talk with _____ who has pertinent information. If I run into any roadblocks, I'll check with you immediately and in any event, I'll give you update reports every week until the job is completed. When I turn in the completed work, I'll appreciate your feedback."

Practice this. It will help you and will also train your boss, if he has been dumping on you.

Successful people — winners at work — ask for help and information. They have an insatiable appetite for learning and growth.

"The price of success is hard work, dedication to the job at hand, and the determination that whether we win or lose, we have applied the best of ourselves to the task at hand."

Vince Lombardi

KEY #11
ASSIST OTHERS IN THEIR RESPONSIBILITIES WHENEVER POSSIBLE

Withhold not good from them to who it is due, when it is in the power of thine hand to do it.

Proverbs 3:27

Those who know me well are aware that I have three important lifetime goals. One of these goals is to put 120 young men through Bible college. I want to do that because I am very interested in the development of young ministers.

A part of that goal is to take ten of the most promising of these young preachers and launch their ministries: financially, emotionally, mentally and physically. I want to do everything in my power to assist these young men become established during the first three years of their ministry.

I get such satisfaction from this type of activity. It is not a burden to me, it is pure joy. I would rather talk to ten young enthusiastic, aspiring preachers than to a listless audience of ten thousand people.

I derive great joy from success — whether it is my own success or the success of others I can help along the way.

Not long ago, one of the young men I am currently assisting called me to share a bit of wonderful news. Based on some information we were able to provide him, he had been able to triple his income in a period of only ninety days. Naturally, he was ecstatic. He had used his new wealth to hire a secretary and to begin drawing up and mailing out newsletters. As a result, he had begun to receive financial assistance beyond his wildest imagination. He was beside himself with excitement and enthusiasm.

I cannot tell you the pleasure that kind of thing gives me. The reason I can't tell you is because it is something you have to experience for yourself to fully appreciate.

There is something phenomenal that happens on the inside when you assist others to attain their dreams and reach their goals. I urge you — for your own sake as well as the sake of others — learn to help those around you on the job and in your daily activities and associations.

I exhort you to think of ways to be an advantage to others in need. What you contribute to their efforts, whether in time or energy or money, may seem like a small thing to you, but I guarantee that you will be amazed at the favor it will generate in that climate — in your office or shop or classroom.

I believe in success-making. I believe that what you make happen for someone else, God will make happen for you. You don't reap *where* you sow, you reap *what* you sow.

In the Bible we read of the trials and tribulations that Job had to endure because of his faithfulness to God. The Scriptures tell us that in the end . . .**the Lord turned the captivity of Job, when he prayed for his friends: also the Lord gave Job twice as much as he had before** (Job 42:10). Pray for your friends, associates and superiors — then see what God will do to turn your captivity and reward your efforts.

I believe with all my heart that if you will become a successmaker, if you will concentrate on assisting others around you, you will literally surround yourself with success.

I have learned that when I help others in my circle of influence to become successful, I am caught up in the midst of their own momentum. I know from personal experience the validity of the phenomenal secret found in Ephesians 6:8:...*that whatsoever good thing any man doeth, the same shall he receive of the Lord....*

Unfortunately, this principle also works in the negative: whatsoever bad thing any man does, the same shall he receive. For example, in the Old Testament Book of Genesis we read how Jacob deceived his aged father into conferring upon him the birthright that rightfully belonged to his elder brother, Esau. Later on, Jacob's father-in-law Laban deceived Jacob by marrying him off to his plain daughter Leah when Jacob really thought he was being wed to the lovely Rachel.

That kind of thing is recorded throughout the pages of Scripture and of history. It is as true in the physical realm as in the spiritual realm that what you sow is what you reap.

The old adage that God helps those who help themselves is not Scripturally accurate. The truth is that God helps those who help others.

If you want to be a success, then learn to assist others to reach their goals and dreams. As you help them meet their duties and responsibilities, the Lord will do the same for you.

You have His Word on it!

"Success consists of a series of little daily efforts."

Mami McCulloch

KEY #12
PROJECT JESUS IN GENUINE LOVE AND ENTHUSIASM.

The servant of the Lord must not strive; but be gentle unto all men, apt to teach, patient,

In meekness instructing those that oppose themselves if God peradventure will give them repentance to the acknowledging of the truth

2 Timothy 2:24,25

As Christians, you and I are obligated by our experience with the Lord to create what I call "a climate of Jesus" around us. That means we must make it possible for people to see Jesus in us and to be drawn to Him — wherever we may be, at home or at work .

However, that does not mean that we are obligated or even expected to try to cram Jesus down people's throats.

I have heard believers who said that they were fired because they were witnessing on the job. My instant reaction to that claim is, "No, they lost their job because they were lousy employees."

I don't think anyone in the United States of America ever gets fired for being a Christian. People get fired for taking their employer's time to witness.

Many Christians seem to have the mistaken idea that they are supposed to go into the stores and shops and classrooms of this nation to force a religious tract into everybody's hand, give them a paperback book, or play a Christian recording for them. If you feel called of the Lord to do that sort of thing, fine — just do it on your own time, not your employer's.

Personally, I believe that Jesus should be projected by our very presence. I encourage you to avoid the religious verbiage that many use as a substitute for holy living. Show an interest in others equal to the interest Jesus showed to everyone He met. Be accessible as an encourager. Be kind as a cushion against the blows of life. Be a harbor from the storms others face that no one else ever discusses. Be strong as an oak so that when others are weak and weary from the heat of the day, you provide a place of shade, rest and comfort.

You will never be a success on the job or off, as a worker or as a believer, if you come across as dogmatic, overbearing, or domineering. Learn to be an ambassador for Christ, not a high-pressure door-to-door salesman. As the old saying goes, "Christianity is more often caught than taught. "

The world is a dark and lonely place for many people. When you project Christ appropriately through your work and actions, you show the people around you a new way — one on which they can depend as never before.

"Winners will take care of themselves. When you give your best effort, that is what makes you a winner."

John Wooden

KEY #13
DO NOT SPREAD GARBAGE
Whoso keepeth his mouth and his tongue keepeth his soul from troubles.
Proverbs 21:23

If you want to be a success, don't try to build yourself up by tearing someone else down.

Successful people do not spread garbage on the job. They don't circulate trash.

Consequently, to succeed, you must tend to yourself, your own business, and let others do the same. Keep a guard on your mouth and your tongue and you will keep yourself out of trouble and strife.

James tells us, **Speak not evil one of another, brethren. He that speaketh evil of his brother, and judgeth his brother, speaketh evil of the law, and judgeth the law: but if thou judge the law, thou art not a doer of the law, but a judge** (James 4:11). In the very next verse he asks, **...who art thou that judgest another?** (James 4:12).

These same words are echoed by the Apostle Paul who asks, **Who art thou that judgest another man's servant? to his own master he standeth or falleth...** (Rom. 14:4). It is dangerous business to set yourself up as judge of another man's servant.

Harness your words. Control your emotions. Don't get involved in anything other than restoration. Only fools get involved with the destruction of others. Champions restore, nurture, encourage.

Instead of spreading stories, do your best to suppress them, even if you know they are true. In Proverbs 17:9 wise Solomon points out: **He that covereth a transgression seeketh love; but he that repeateth a matter separateth very friends.** Then in Proverbs 18:8 he notes: **The words of a talebearer are as wounds, and they go down into the innermost part of the belly.** If you want to spare yourself and others from much grief and pain, then set a watch on your lips.

I thank God for a staff that does not "bad mouth" each another. One reason I am so grateful for such people is because I am convinced that if they will talk bad about one another to me, they will talk bad about me to one another.

One of the greatest ways to prove your capacity for loyalty is for others to discover that you refuse to make any derogatory statements regarding people not present. Cultivate these three habits:

1) Be loyal to those not present.

2) Be loyal to those not present.

3) BE LOYAL TO THOSE NOT PRESENT.

You are the seed that gives birth to the atmosphere around you. As you create an atmosphere of integrity, peace and stability, you prevent slander of others in your presence . . .**discover not a secret to another: Lest he that heareth it put thee to shame, and thine infamy turn not way** (Prov. 25:9,10).

Don't be a talebearer, a gossipmonger or a troublemaker. Don't waste your time and your employer's time carrying tales and spreading rumors. Instead, give your best effort to your labor and watch for the Lord to reward you with His best effort on your behalf.

"Happiness lies in the joy of achievement and the thrill of creative effort."

Franklin Delano Roosevelt

KEY #14
PROJECT AN ATTITUDE OF FORGIVENESS, MERCY AND FAVOR ON YOUR JOB
Blessed are the merciful: for they shall obtain mercy.
Matthew 5:7

If you would like to be viewed as a happy, competent, knowledgeable, creative and successful person, then learn to project an attitude of forgiveness, mercy, and favor. Believe me, this is a tall order. To practice this lifestyle means that you must climb higher up the ladder of wisdom to see further ahead.

In James 3:17,18 we are told that . . .**the wisdom that is from above is first pure, then peaceable, gentle, and easy to be intreated, full of mercy and good fruits, without partiality, and without hypocrisy. And the fruit of righteousness is sown in peace of them that make peace.**

Mercy is not just an action, it is an attitude. Mercy is not expressed in the idea that "I will forgive you this time, but woe unto you if you ever do it again!" Mercy is interpreting another person's weakness in the light of our own.

The Bible exhorts us to show mercy one to another: . . .**be ye kind one to another, tenderhearted, forgiving one another, even as God for Christ's sake hath forgiven you** (Eph. 4:32).

The person who is merciful and forgiving and who shows favor to others will receive the same of the Lord Who has promised happiness, prosperity and success to all those who receive and show forth His nature in them.

Forgiveness marks you as Christ's. Mercy welds hearts together. Favor forges unforgettable bonds. Isaiah 58:10-12 teaches that if you reach out to an afflicted soul, God will turn on your own light in your nighttime!

Think long term. Joseph did. While in prison, he interpreted a butler's dream. The butler was later restored to fellowship and favor with the Pharaoh. Two years passed before he remembered Joseph. When he did, it was the beginning of a radical change for Joseph. Think of it — from the prison to the palace!

We never know when the mercy, forgiveness and favor that we show another will come back to us. In this attitude, we project our decision to bless the world around us.

Create a climate that attracts others. God will see to it that you are honored and even promoted.

In the foreword to his book, *The Magic of Thinking Big,* David Schwartz said:

"Our six year old son, David, felt mighty big when he was graduating from kindergarten. I asked him what he planned to be when he finished growing up. Davy looked at me intently for a moment and then answered, 'Dad, I want to be a professor.'

'A professor? A professor of what?' I asked.

'Well, dad,' he replied, 'I think I want to be a professor of happiness'."

78

This little lad had already learned a big secret in life: be aggressively happy! I can't think of a greater assignment in life, can you?

"If a man is called to be a streetsweeper, he should sweep streets even as Michelangelo painted, or Beethoven composed music, or Shakespeare wrote poetry. He should sweep streets so well that all the host of heaven and earth will pause to say, Here lived a great streetsweeper who did his job well."

Martin Luther King, Jr.

KEY #15
DO MORE THAN IS EXPECTED OF YOU
*And whosoever shall compel thee to go a mile,
go with him twain.*
Matthew 5:41

Have you ever been in a restaurant and asked the waitress to do some little extra service such as bringing you some sauce for your steak? How did she respond? Did she react as though you had asked her to volunteer for a suicide mission? Or did she give the impression that it was a joy and a pleasure to be of special assistance to you?

Just recently my staff and I were eating in a restaurant and were amazed at the friendly, courteous, willing service we received from our waitress. She kept coming back to the table asking what she could do for us to make our meal more enjoyable. She was continually bringing tea, pouring coffee, filling the water glasses, taking away dirty dishes, suggesting delicious desserts. Naturally, when we were finished with our meal, we left a generous tip. Why? Because of her attitude. She seemed delighted to "go the second mile."

As Christians, that is what you and I are to do in our service to our employer as well as to our fellow man.

That attitude of willingness to do more than is required or expected is what I look for in a potential employee. In fact, I watch for it daily among my staff and make sure that those who display it are amply rewarded with extra incentives such as salary raises, increased benefits, and additional time off. I give them extra lee-way and advantages because they give me extra effort.

Whatever your line of work, you will find that it pays to do more than you have to do, more than is required or expected of you.

J. Willard Marriott, founder of the Marriott Corporation, was known to work eighteen hours a day for many years. "No person can get very far in this life on a forty-hour week," he said. Harvey McKay, author of *Beware the Naked Man Who Offers You His Shirt*, says, "Don't try to meet your quotas. Exceed them."

Exceeding quotas and expectations accomplishes three very important things:

1) It gives your creativity a chance to soar. I read the other day that on a bingo card of ninety numbers, there are approxi-mately forty-four million possible ways to make "Bingo." So it is with life. Be willing to do more than is expected and your results will match the effort. You'll discover things you had not seen before. You won't be trapped in the rut of sameness and boredom like thousands of others.

2) It causes those around you to raise their own level of per-formance. When Roger Bannister ran the mile in four minutes, he overcame huge obstacles. He, and all the runners before him, had repeatedly been told by many experts that it was physically impossible for a human being to run a mile in four minutes. However, he became convinced in his mind that he could do it. He constantly trained his mind and body to that end. Consequently, he became a "first." Now, many hundreds of athletes run the mile in four minutes and less every year. By doing more than was expected, he set a new standard.

3) It gives tangible evidence of your walk with Christ. Scripture tells us that Jesus . . .**went about doing good.** . . (Acts 10:38). We have many examples of His willingness to go beyond the expectations of those around Him. The Apostle Paul said in First Corinthians 15:10, **But by the grace of God I am what I am . . .but I labored more abundantly than they all: yet not I, but the grace of God which was with me.** Believe me, others take note of the man or woman who, without need of recognition but for the sheer joy of service and excellence, steps beyond just what is expected.

"I recall the story of the farmer who, when asked by his neighbor why he was working his sons so hard just to grow corn, he replied, 'I'm not just growing corn, I'm growing sons.'"

Kenneth Blanchard

KEY #16
LEARN TO HARNESS YOUR ANGER AND CONTROL YOUR SPIRIT

He that hath no rule over his own spirit is like a city that is broken down, and without walls.

Proverbs 25:28

Anger has energy.

Anger can be deadly.

Anger is often the result of focus on the wrong things.

Anger puts people in prison, explodes marriages, destroys friendships.

Let me share an example with you from my own experience.

When I was a young man, just beginning in the ministry, over a certain period of time I was asked to preach crusades in five major churches, some of the largest in our movement. At the time, the financial situation in each of those churches was shaky. As a result, instead of being given a share of the offerings from the meetings, I was provided a set salary — in each case, much less than I expected.

By the time I began to preach in the fifth church, I was cocked and primed and ready for a change.

The week-long crusade I preached was tremendous with a great response both spiritually and materially. Sure enough, at the end of the week, the pastor came and brought me a check. It was for $350.

I was so disappointed and upset that I cried for two hours. I was sure that I was being cheated and taken advantage of by unscrupulous people. I told the Lord, "Father, I'd rather work for con men in the world than con men in the Church."

You may not have realized it yet, but the work of the Lord is not always full of pure and holy people in every sense of the word. That revelation was a shock to me at first.

I was so distraught by what I believed to be unfair and dishonest treatment by the Lord's servants that I was ready to leave the ministry and go to work in the secular realm.

Fortunately, a friend came to me and reminded me of the passage in Matthew 5:23,24 in which Jesus taught that if we have a problem between us and our brother we should go to him and resolve it. So, I went to talk to the pastor — who, incidentally, was not dishonest and later became a trusted and valued friend.

"Brother, were you dissatisfied with the revival?" I asked him.

"Oh, no, Mike," he assured me. "Everything went just fine. I was very pleased. Why do you ask? Did you feel that something was wrong?"

"Yes, I did," I answered sharply, "the offering."

"Oh?" he replied. "How much did you want, a thousand dollars for the week?"

"No," I told him with a sour tone. "I wanted *all* the offerings. God may have meant for me to have three thousand dollars. Whatever came in, that's what I want."

I was angry and bitter, and the pastor could tell it. He was kind and gentle and soothing and offered me another check, which I took without a word of thanks.

"God bless you," he said as I left.

I got what I asked for, but I was not invited back to that church for five long years. I also suffered in other ways. The pastor told some other ministers what I had done, and soon the word got around. It took quite a while for me to live down that episode, and the reputation I got as a result of it.

From that bitter experience, I learned an important lesson: One harsh statement, one rash act, one moment of unbridled passion can unravel years of work and preparation. One phrase spoken out of place, one emotion allowed out of control can ruin a relationship. And the relationships and friendships that God provides for us are more precious than any paycheck, no matter how large it may be.

Through the years I have learned to value friendships above all else. I have also set my mind and heart and will to learn to harness my anger and control my spirit. It has not always been easy — and is not always easy even now. There have been times when I have had to almost kick out windows to keep myself from kicking off somebody's head. But windows can be replaced, friends can't.

Remember: One true friend is more valuable than any amount of "filthy lucre."

The writer of the Book of Proverbs tells us, **He that is soon angry dealeth foolishly. . . .** (Prov. 14:17), but, **He that is slow to anger is better than the mighty; and he that ruleth his spirit than he that taketh a city** (Prov. 16:32).

No matter how holy and sanctified you may be, you will never be all that the Lord requires of you or that man expects of you until you have learned to harness your anger and control your spirit.

"He who masters his time, masters his life."

Mike Murdock

KEY #17
KEEP ACCURATE RECORDS
*Be thou diligent to know the state of thy flocks,
and look well to thy herds.*
Proverbs 27:23

Accurate record keeping is the basis of all successful business.

Like so many other lessons of life, I have had to learn that truth the hard way.

I hate to keep records. To be perfectly honest, I have despised it from childhood, although I have learned through the years that according to God's established structure I must give an account of myself and my actions.

Naturally, given my temperament and personality, I don't like keeping track of all the hundreds of details involved in my ministry and my personal finances. If it were possible, I would send the Internal Revenue Service one lump-sum payment today and never have to deal with them again in my lifetime.

I hate having to keep receipts of every meal I eat and every item I purchase. In fact, I find record keeping of any type tedious, tiring, laborious, frustrating and time-consuming. But I have also found that it is the best way to validate integrity, which is how I have had to learn to look at it rather than simply as a means of satisfying the government.

I urge you to learn to keep accurate records. Work out a system for everything you do. You will find that in the long run it will pay rich dividends by saving time, energy, and money. It is also the best way to preserve relationships and protect friendships.

King Solomon counseled us to look to the state of our flocks and our herds. He knew how important it is to know what we have, where we got it, and what is being done with it. That's not just good business practice, it is good stewardship.

Here are some useful tips that I have found beneficial:

1) Have a place for your receipts and staple them to file-sized paper before filing. Often, the receipts from credit cards, restaurants, gasoline stations are small and can easily be lost in a shuffle of papers, paper clips, stuffed file cabinets.

2) Have a table of contents (chart of accounts) for retrieving all receipts and information when necessary.

3) When dealing with paper work, remember to touch it only once. Use the T.R.A.F. rule:

Throw it away instantly if it serves no purpose for your goals.

Refer it or delegate it and mark you calendar for follow-up.

Act immediately if it will benefit you or others who depend on you.

File it NOW. Don't "pile" it.

Whether we like it or not, both God and man will hold us

responsible and accountable. No one will be successful in this life or the next who has not learned to exercise diligence in every service.

"Give me a stock clerk
with a goal and I will give
you a man who will
make history. Give me a man
without a goal and I will
give you a stock clerk."

J.C. Penney

KEY #18

AVOID FLATTERY AND DO NOT GIVE UNDESERVED PRAISE

As he that bindeth a stone in a sling, so is he that giveth honour to a fool....

Proverbs 26:8,28

I realize that this key goes against much of what is being taught and practiced in modern society both inside and outside the Church. There is a current popular emphasis on positive thought, outlook and reinforcement. The truth is that I just don't believe in lying, even if it is for a good cause or with the best of intentions.

I don't believe in telling someone that he is great when he isn't. I don't believe in telling a musician that he sang or played well if he didn't. I don't believe in telling a preacher that his sermon was marvelous and that it spoke directly to my heart, if that was not the case.

There is far too much flattery in our society today. When you and I start giving honor where is it not due and praise where it is not deserved, we begin to destroy our credibility.

I believe in being positive, but I also believe in being honest. I believe it is possible to encourage and uplift others by our words, but I also believe that those words must be spoken in truth and love.

I believe that it is possible to find something good in every person and every situation. However, there is nothing cheaper than shallow words, intended only to manipulate or impress.

My staff knows me. They know that if they do well, I will be the first to acknowledge it. I will do everything in my power to encourage and uplift those who give their time and energy in my behalf. At the same time, they also know that I will not tell them they have done well when they haven't. They know I will not flatter them. If they make a mistake, I won't dismiss it with, "Oh, who cares?" I care, and I let them know it.

For example, if one of my staff members is not a good telephone conversationalist, rather than telling him how terrific he is on the phone, I will be honest enough to acknowledge that speaking on the wire is not his best gift. I will then find what his best gift is and help him to make optimum use of it.

My staff will tell you that they always know exactly where they stand with me. If I tell them that they are good at something, they know it is true and not just so much flattery to make them feel good about themselves or to hype them into doing something they really don't like to do or don't feel suited for.

Now I am not advocating undue harshness or cruelty of speech or manner. I hope you will cultivate the ability to see and freely acknowledge the good in everyone you deal with. But I also hope that you will learn to avoid lying lips.

Don't give honor where it is not due or praise where it is not deserved. Not only is it dishonest, it is counterproductive. It is also destructive to your own reputation.

One time an individual began to brag on me, telling me what a wonderful speaker I was. I was thrilled. It felt so good to be told that I was an excellent communicator — until I heard the same person say the same thing about someone else using the same identical words. Immediately his words lost their value to me. After that experience I had no confidence whatsoever in what that person had to say about me or anyone else.

I lost respect for that individual because he had demonstrated to me that he was not honest and sincere. I might have been tempted to make allowances for him if he had given praise to someone I knew deserved it, but he didn't. I knew that what he was saying was just empty verbiage, just so many words spoken in an obvious attempt to generate attention.

Make your words count. Don't say that someone or something is fabulous unless it is the truth. Don't use flattery or give undeserved praise. Instead, learn to speak the truth in wisdom and in love.

"It has been my observation
that most people get ahead
during the time that
others waste."

Henry Ford

KEY #19

REFUSE THE BONDAGE OF BRIBERY AND THE INFLUENCE OF INTIMIDATION

A wicked man taketh a gift out of the bosom to pervert the ways of judgment.

Proverbs 17:23

Be not afraid of their faces: for I am with thee to deliver thee, saith the Lord.

Jeremiah 1:8

Satan always tries to offer a substitute for God's real thing. As beautiful as giving is, it can be perverted into bribery and thereby turned into something evil, something to destroy people's lives.

Giving can be used to create within people a sense of bondage. Let me give you some examples: The businessman who buys you an exceptional gift to get you to keep doing business with him. The boss who does something spectacular to influence you to cover up what he doesn't want others to find out. The employer who provides you extra pay or benefits in exchange for your help in an undertaking he knows is illegal or unethical.

There is a great deal of this type of activity going on today in the business world. You will find that many people in commerce and industry as well as in politics and government use giving as a means of controlling the lives of others. They make use of gifts to influence others and to bind them to themselves.

If you are to be successful in this life, you must be sensitive in this crucial area.

If you know that your boss is lying on his income tax because he offers you a special gift to win your favor and influence your testimony on his behalf, what he is doing is perverting your judgment.

My brother is in business and he tells me that kickbacks are a common practice among the salesmen in his particular field.

I know of a well-known and respected businessman in Dallas, Texas, who buys tickets to athletic games to distribute to all his customers as a bid to exercise control over their judgment and opinions.

Now some may claim that such activity is not only general practice today, but that it is accepted practice as well. I disagree. You must be careful or such thinking and acting will destroy you. Although refusing special gifts and favors may be difficult, accepting them will obligate you to the one who offers them. Eventually they will work against you because that person will lose respect for you and may even come to resent and despise you.

As evidence, look at our own nation and its foreign policies. In the past half-century or more the United States of America has made tremendous gifts to countries around the world. As a result, we have created a sense of intimidation among our allies as well as a sense of animosity among our enemies. Many of those nations and peoples we have favored most have eventually turned on us and now hate us and everything for which we stand.

Please do not misunderstand me. There is nothing wrong with giving, when the motive is right. But when the attitude is to give as a means to influence judgment or opinion or control the lives of others, the practice is not only wrong, it is counterproductive — and destructive. It will ultimately destroy both the giver and the one receiving the gift.

If I were to try to use gifts and favors to manipulate my staff, sooner or later I would cause them to turn on me. There is a natural human tendency to develop a distrust and a disgust for those who make us feel obligated to them.

When you are offered undeserved gifts and obvious bribes, refuse them. Don't allow yourself to become intimidated by them or by those who offer them to you. Just because someone has done something nice for you does not mean that you owe that person a favor in return.

I don't believe in doing favors for people. I don't do favors, I give favor. There is a difference — a *big* difference.

A favor is an action designed to link another individual to me.

On the other hand, favor is an attitude of God whereby I give that individual what I have, with no thought of return. When I show favor to an individual, I know that my harvest will come not from that person but from my heavenly Father.

Any time I hear someone say, "So-and-So owes me a favor," I make a note not to have any dealings with that individual. I know that anything he or she does for me will be expected to be repaid — with interest.

My staff will testify that I will not allow myself to become indebted to anyone. By the same token, I will not allow anyone to become indebted to me. As of this moment, no one on this earth owes me a thing in return for what I have done for him or her. If I do something for someone, it is a gift, not a favor.

When you learn to look to the Lord rather than to other people for your harvest, you are set free from the bondage of bribery and the influence of intimidation.

I believe that is one of the reasons I have kept many dear and close friends for years and years. I believe that when friendships are based on mutual respect, admiration, and affection, there is no need to swap favors.

Don't get into the habit of trading meals or other gratuities. Don't take a friend to lunch, and then expect that person to return the favor in the future. And don't allow anyone to do that to you. That kind of mutual obligation destroys the fun and the spontaneity of a friendship and relationship.

If you want to be a success, learn to be a giver.

"The poorest man is not he who is without a cent, but he who is without a dream."

Pennsylvania School Journal

KEY #20

MAKE JESUS CHRIST YOUR DIVINE WORK PARTNER

And, ye masters, do the same things unto them, forbearing threatening: knowing that your Master also is in heaven; neither is there respect of persons with him.

Ephesians 6:9

As we have seen earlier, the Bible speaks of the Holy Spirit as a Counselor, an Advisor, a Companion, as One Who walks beside us.

This passage in Ephesians, which promises us that whatever we do to others, we will receive the same from the Lord, also states that we all serve the same heavenly Master.

I am convinced that God, our heavenly Master, wants to be a part of our working life. He wants to be there with us as we go about fulfilling the demands of our occupation. He wants to help us with the labor of our hands. He wants to share the sweat of our brow, the toil that we expend as we sow our life in diligence toward those around us. He wants to be with us to support and assist us as we give our best for our employer.

When you work for someone else, you are giving that person not only your labor, but also your very existence; not just your body, but also your heart and mind. You are sowing your very life into that job. If you want to be assured of success in that effort, if you want to be assured of the recompense that is due you, then make Jesus Christ not only your Savior and Lord, but also your daily Divine Work Partner.

You may be wondering just how you go about doing that. It is really very simple.

103

First of all, think of Him as your Divine Advisor. Picture Him in your mind as being right there beside you on the job day by day, communing with you, talking to you, showing you how to do your work better and better, inspiring you and giving you increased creativity.

Be sensitive to the leadership of the Holy Spirit Who indwells you.

There are times when I must make difficult decisions I do not always feel qualified or prepared to make. At such times I simply pray, "Holy Spirit, please show me what to do. Lord, what is Your will, Your plan, Your desire in this situation? What should I do?" And in an instant the voice of the Lord will speak on the inside of me and give me the instructions and direction I need.

The Lord is that close to you. Jesus is a Friend Who sticks closer than a brother. So look to Him as your Divine Advisor, as the One Who talks to you and gives you guidance and direction for your life.

Also think of Him as your Divine Counselor, as the One Who gives you insight into the lives of others on your job. Think of Him as showing you how to relate and react to other people around you. Think of Him as giving you revelation knowledge of how to interpret and minister to the needs of others.

You will find that as the Lord begins to speak to your heart, you will begin to discern those around you in a different way. You will sense when they are struggling under stress and unable to perform at top efficiency.

There is another way that you can enlist and maintain Jesus

Christ as your Divine Work Partner. Each morning on your way to work, ask the Lord to make you a more productive worker.

After all, Jesus is the epitome of productivity. He came to this earth to give His life for one purpose — to produce a family, the family of God. As He was dying on Calvary, He cried out, "It is finished!" In essence, what He was saying is, "I have finished My job. I have done My duty. I have fulfilled My divine calling. I have given My life as the Savior of the world. I have been obedient to the instructions of My heavenly Father."

That means that He is sensitive to and aware of your responsibilities.

He knows when you are under pressure.

He knows when you are struggling on your job and in your career.

Let Him go before you to prepare the way for you day by day.

Chapter 3

....

QUESTIONS TO ASK YOURSELF ABOUT YOUR JOB, YOUR TALENTS AND YOUR GIFTS

YOUR SEVEN-QUESTION JOB ANALYSIS

1. Are you really happy with what you are presently doing?

Your personal excitement and enthusiasm about your productivity each day is so important. Nobody else can answer this but YOU.

2. Is your present job actually a short-range or long-range goal?

For instance, high school or college students may not intend to work their entire lifetimes at fast food restaurants. So, their "after school" job is a *short-range goal.* They are gaining education, experience and basic financial provision.

3. Are your God-given gifts and strongest talents being developed?

Prosperity and promotion usually come to those who totally focus on their *most significant skills.*

4. Are you working just to pay your bills and have fun or to truly express a contribution to life and to this world?

Prominent achievers go the extra mile.

5. Do you feel that God is satisfied with what you are doing now?

I remember one tremendous guitarist who left a night club band after honestly answering this question. Though he loved his music, he felt God did not want him sowing his talents in such an environment.

6. Do you feel that you are doing the highest quality of work that you are capable of doing?

Millions cultivate the habit of mediocrity in their daily duties. If you are not striving for total excellence, you either have the wrong job or the wrong *attitude*.

7. Do you feel like you are working "as unto the Lord"?

You must see the work you do for your boss as work you are doing for God. If not, you will soon resent your boss and the time you spend on his work. This attitude will eventually cause you to feel unfulfilled and unproductive.

Seriously consider the above questions. Then, ask the Lord for His instructions regarding your career.

HOW TO DETERMINE WHAT YOU REALLY WANT IN A JOB

1. How much income do you personally feel that you need to consider yourself financially successful?

Each of us has different needs. Some have 5 X 7 dreams. Other have 16 X 20 dreams. Neither is right or wrong. The key is to establish a true picture of your personal desires.

2. What kind of problems do you really love to solve?

You can determine this by your favorite topic of conversation, favorite books and magazines that you enjoy. What would you *enjoy* about this *the most? These things reveal your true interests.*

3. What kind of environment do you find most enjoyable?

Some people discover that they need many people around them to be most productive. Others prefer solitude.

4. What are your social needs?

If your job deprives you of important relationships, it will become a source of discomfort and depression. You must diagnose your personal leisure and social needs that your happiness requires.

5. What kind of family life or time do you feel necessary for you?

Obviously, a bachelor schedules his life differently from a family man with five children or a divorced mother of an infant. The job that is right for you should provide adequate time for sharing with those you love.

6. What level of social approval and respect do you need?

Each of us wants to be accepted by our friends. Never work for a company of which you are ashamed.

One man admitted to me that he had no confidence in the products he was promoting. Consequently, he experienced very little success. He left that job and went to work with a company he could honestly support. *It made all the difference in the world.*

7. What kind of financial future is necessary for your peace of mind?

While very few jobs offer a lifetime guarantee, every one of us needs a sense of predictable income. *Tomorrow does come.*

Four Rewards Your Work Should Provide For You

1. A sense of worth, pride and significance

Never speak lightly of your job if it produces a sense of worthiness or fulfillment, and is something that you truly believe in.

2. A sense of achievement and progress

You should feel that there is a real need for what you are doing. . .that you are providing something worthwhile for other people.

Productivity is vital for happiness. *Other people should benefit from something that you are doing every day.*

3. A sense of personal growth

Your mind should be expanding, stretching and developing each day. Some people even change careers in the middle of their lives because of the monotony and boredom their routines produce.

4. Sufficient finances to provide adequately for your needs and those you love

The Apostle Paul wrote, **But if any provide not for his own, and specially for those of his own house, he hath denied the faith, and is worse than an infidel** (1 Tim. 5:8).

It is vital that you honestly answer these questions before you can successfully release the four important forces that guarantee career success.

Set aside at least thirty minutes right now to write out detailed answers. The results may amaze you and set in motion a significant change in your future.

Chapter 4

TIPS FOR BECOMING ORGANIZED IN THE WORKPLACE

THE BASICS OF GETTING ORGANIZED

1. Set priorities.

The first step in getting organized is setting your priorities, deciding what needs to be done first, or what is most important.

Also, this is not a one-time task. Setting priorities is a continuous, every-day process.

2. Develop a plan.

Whether it is a long-range goal or a day's work, plan how to get there or to get the things done that need doing — then *stick to your plan,* barring unforeseen circumstances that have to be dealt with.

In that case, deal with the emergency or interruption as quickly as possible, then get back to your plan.

3. Do not attempt to do everything at once.

Take one thing at a time — one minute at a time, one hour at a time, one day at a time.

Letting yourself be overwhelmed with an entire project will trigger your body's alarm system. The result will be stress and possibly burnout or physical problems.

Develop a system for filing things to work on later.

Make secondary lists.

See what can be given to someone else to do or what can be eliminated completely as not absolutely necessary.

4. Make sure you have the tools you need.

If you need a typewriter computer, filing cabinets, a desk, storage space, and so forth, arrange to get those things in order of priority.

5. Organize your work space.

Your work space should be adequate and comfortable, at least.

It should have proper seating — a good, comfortable chair with back support; ventilation — without adequate oxygen, you get sleepy, and lighting — eyestrain causes headaches at first and eye problems later.

6. Organize your desk.

If you are re-organizing your desk, better set aside a certain amount of time to deal with this; if you are arranging a new desk, the task is easier.

a. Throw away everything that is no longer of any use. Ask yourself these questions:

"What is the worst thing that can happen if I throw this away?"

"When is the last time I used it?"

b.   Periodically review your files, keeping only the current, essential ones in your desk. More than ninety percent of all files more than a year old are never used again.

c.   Get trays for "input" and "output."

d.   Once you have your desk organized, keep only what you are working on in sight.

e.   Keep items off your desk until you are ready for them. Otherwise, you may be distracted from the main project by something more fun or something that can be done easier. That will throw off your priorities and create snowballing problems as the time goes on.

f.   Keep a pad or notebook handy in which to jot down ideas as they come to you. Writing down ideas not only ensures that you will remember them but helps clarify them in your mind.

g.   Do not do anything at your desk that is not work. Do not let it become a place to socialize. If you develop the habit of working in a certain place, you will find yourself getting down to business much more rapidly when it is time to work.

15 TOP TIME-WASTERS

Experience in fourteen countries with managers at various levels in diverse organizations led to a clear picture of time-wasters that afflict managers generally. In everyone's list, five things ranked at or near the top. They are:

1.   Telephone interruptions.

2.   Drop-in visitors.

3.   Meetings (scheduled and unscheduled).

4. Crises.

5. Lack of objectives, priorities, and deadlines.

These five were followed closely by another group of five time thieves:

6. Cluttered desk and personal disorganization.

7. Ineffective delegation and personal involvement in routine affairs and small details.

8. Attempting too much at once, unrealistic time estimates.

9. Confused chains of authority and responsibility.

10. Inadequate, inaccurate, or delayed information.

Depending upon the group, particular leadership styles, and organizational characteristics, other time-wasters often included another set of five things:

11. Indecision and procrastination.

12. Lack of, or unclear, communication and instructions.

13. Inability to say "no."

14. Lack of controls, standards, and progress reports to keep track of the completion of tasks.

15. Fatigue and lack of self-discipline.

It would be profitable for you to sit down and make your own list to give you a starting point for eliminating personal time-wasters.

Take a typical day, list everything you do — even telephone calls, visits to the bathroom, and time for "breaks" or lunch — then go over the list to see what could have been eliminated. Be ruthless in marking time wasters.

A man's time, when well-husbanded, is like
a cultivated field,
of which a few acres produces more
of what is useful to life
than extensive provinces,
even of the richest soil
when overrun with weeds and brambles.

David Hume

TIPS FOR MAKING SCHEDULES

In laying out a weekly schedule, the key is to block out time for top-priority jobs:

■ Reserve a particular day of the week — say Tuesday or Tuesday morning — for major projects.

■ Even if your schedule is broken up with interruptions, you can attempt to keep certain blocks of time intact for high-value priorities.

Remember: *there is always enough time for the important things.*

■ Trying to do the same thing at the same time each day conserves and generates energy.

You have two kinds of "prime time."

■ *Internal prime time* is when you know you work the best, whether it is morning or afternoon.

117

■ *External prime time* is the best time to attend to other people, those you must deal with either on the job, socially, or at home.

Try to save external time for prime projects.

■ Build flexibility into your schedule.

1. Reserve an hour a day that is uncommitted.

2. Leave holes for interviews, conversations, or whatever else that may run longer than scheduled.

3. Set aside time to read the mail and catch up on paperwork.

■ Do not neglect your personal life. Build in time for this as well.

Many men who make their personal lives subordinate to their careers fail in the end. I have seen this with athletes who are great leaders on the sports fields, but who fail to lead in many areas of their home lives.

This is frustrating to their wives, causes bitterness, and short-changes their children. In other words, it is unfair to your wife and children when they are not included in your priorities.

■ Do not put in too many hours of overtime.

The more overtime a person puts in, the more exhausted he is, and the less efficient he becomes. The answer is not to spend more time on a project, but to work more effectively in the time allotted.

You cannot work as effectively if you are fatigued from excessive hours.

When it is built into your schedule properly, doing nothing is not a waste of time.

■ Schedule time to relax among your priorities.

If you arrange things so that you have time to relax and do nothing, you will not only get more done but have more fun doing it!

When I first started in the life insurance business, I was excited about the fact that I could work seven days a week as many hours as I wished.

However, as I began to cut my selling time to five days and then to four, I found I was able to do more business than when I had the whole week stretched out in front of me to see people any time of the day or evening.

■ Use the time you do have more wisely.

Why spend two hours at lunch, when back in the office, the phones are quiet and other people are gone?

Eat quickly and lightly — which also will keep you from getting sleepy or tired in the afternoon — and use that time to get things done that need concentration.

If you are a homemaker, use the time when the children are at school or taking naps.

If you are an employer, allow your people to read, write, or whatever after their scheduled work is done.

You cannot push people to be creative by the clock. Beyond a certain point, simply putting in hours is not the best way to get creative work done.

Unless you schedule time for relaxation or creativity, you will never have it.

If you allow it, there will always be enough work to spill over into any free time.

Work does expand to fill the time available.

Parkinson's Law

In addition to scheduling enough periods of relaxation during the week, it pays in the long run to take a look tow or three months ahead, see what is planned, and set the time aside on a monthly or a quarterly basis to take an extended period of time off. Perhaps it is just a long weekend, but it will pay off in increased efficiency over the long run.

Chapter 5

....

INSPIRATION AND MOTIVATION FOR THE WORKPLACE

SCRIPTURE GUIDES FOR DILIGENT WORK

The following Scripture quotations are taken from the
Holy Bible, New International Version.

Lazy hands make a man poor, but diligent hands bring wealth.

He who gathers crops in summer is a wise son, but he who sleeps during harvest is a disgraceful son.

Proverbs 10:4,5

The wages of the righteous bring them life, but the income of the wicked brings them punishment.

Proverbs 10:16

He who works his land will have abundant food, but he who chases fantasies lacks judgment.

Proverbs 12:11

From the fruit of his lips a man is filled with good things as surely as the work of his hands rewards him.

Proverbs 12:14

Diligent hands will rule, but laziness ends in slave labor.

Proverbs 12:24

The lazy man does not roast his game, but the diligent man prizes his possessions.

Proverbs 12:27

The sluggard craves and gets nothing, but the desires of the diligent are fully satisfied.

Proverbs 13:4

Dishonest money dwindles away, but he who gathers money little by little makes it grow.

Proverbs 13:11

All hard work brings a profit, but mere talk leads only to poverty.

Proverbs 14:23

One who is slack in his work is brother to one who destroys.

Proverbs 18:9

Laziness brings on deep sleep, and the shiftless man goes hungry.

Proverbs 19:15

The sluggard buries his hand in the dish; he will not even bring it back to his mouth!

Proverbs 19:24

A sluggard does not plow in season; so at harvest time he looks but finds nothing.

Proverbs 20:4

Do not love sleep or you will grow poor; stay awake and you will have food to spare.

Proverbs 20:13

The plans of the diligent lead to profit as surely as haste leads to poverty.

Proverbs 21:5

The sluggard's craving will be the death of him, because his hands refuse to work.

All day long he craves for more, but the righteous give without sparing.

Proverbs 21:25,26

Do you see a man skilled in his work? He will serve before kings; he will not serve before obscure men.

Proverbs 22:29

I went past the field of the sluggard, past the vineyard of the man who lacks judgment;

Thorns had come up everywhere, the ground was covered with weeds, and the stone wall was in ruins.

I applied my heart to what I observed and learned a lesson from what I saw:

A little sleep, a little slumber, a little folding of the hands to rest—

And poverty will come on you like a bandit and scarcity like an armed man.

Proverbs 24:30-34

Be sure you know the condition of your flocks, give careful attention to your herds.

Proverbs 27:23

He who works his land will have abundant food, but the one who chases fantasies will have his fill of poverty.

A faithful man will be richly blessed, but one eager to get rich will not go unpunished.

Proverbs 28:19,20

That everyone may eat and drink, and find satisfaction in all his toil — this is the gift of God.

Ecclesiastes 3:13

Moreover, when God gives any man wealth and possessions, and enables him to enjoy them, to accept his lot and be happy in his work — this is a gift of God.

Ecclesiastes 5:19

If a man is lazy, the rafters sag; if his hands are idle, the house leaks.

Ecclesiastes 10:18

Be devoted to one another in brotherly love. Honor one another above yourselves.

Never be lacking in zeal, but keep your spiritual fervor, serving the Lord.

Romans 12:10,11

He who has been stealing must steal no longer, but must work, doing something useful with his own hands, that he may have something to share with those in need.

Ephesians 4:28

Slaves, obey your earthly masters with respect and fear, and with sincerity of heart, just as you would obey Christ.

Obey them not only to win their favor when their eye is on you, but like slaves of Christ, doing the will of God from your heart.

Serve wholeheartedly, as if you were serving the Lord, not men,

because you know that the Lord will reward everyone for whatever good he does, whether he is slave or free.

Ephesians 6:5-8

Slaves, obey your earthly masters in everything; and do it not only when their eye is on you and to win their favor, but with sincerity of heart and reverence for the Lord.

Whatever you do, work at it with all your heart, as working for the Lord, not for men.

Colossians 3:22,23

Make it your ambition to lead a quiet life, to mind your own business and to work with your hands, just as we told you,

so that your daily life may win the respect of outsiders and so that you will not be dependent on anybody.

1 Thessalonians 4:11,12

For even when we were with you, we gave you this rule: "If a man will not work, he shall not eat."

2 Thessalonians 3:10

Chapter 6

FOR THE ENTREPRENEUR AND BUSINESS OWNER

TEN RULES FOR BUILDING A BUSINESS
By Sam Walton, Founder, Wal-Mart

Rule 1: COMMIT to your business. Believe in it more than anybody else. I think I overcame every single one of my personal shortcomings by the sheer passion I brought to my work. I don't know if you're born with this kind of passion or if you can learn it. But I do know you need it. If you love your work, you'll be out there every day trying to do it the best you possibly can, and pretty soon everybody around will catch the passion from you — like a fever.

Rule 2: SHARE your profits with all your associates, and treat them as partners. In turn, they will treat you as a partner, and together you will all perform beyond your wildest expectations. Remain a corporation and retain control if you like, but behave as a servant leader in partnership. Encourage your associates to hold a stake in the company. Offer discounted stock and grant them stock for their retirement. It's the single best thing we ever did.

Rule 3: **MOTIVATE** your partners. Money and ownership alone aren't enough. Constantly, day by day, think of new and more interesting ways to motivate and challenge your partners. Set high goals, encourage competition, and then keep score. Make bets with outrageous payoffs. If things get stale, cross-pollinate; have managers switch jobs with one another to stay challenged. Keep everybody guessing as to what your next trick is going to be. Don't become too predictable.

Rule 4: **COMMUNICATE** everything you possibly can to your partners. The more they know, the more they'll understand. The more they understand, the more they'll care. Once they care, there's no stopping them. If you don't trust your associates to know what's going on, they'll know you don't really consider them partners. Information is power, and the gain you get from empowering your associates more than offsets the risk of informing your competitors.

Rule 5: **APPRECIATE** everything your associates do for the business. A paycheck and a stock option will buy one kind of loyalty. But all of us like to be told how much somebody appreciates what we do for them. We like to hear it often, and especially when we have done something we're really proud of. Nothing else can quite substitute for a few well-chosen, well-timed, sincere words of praise. They're absolutely free — and worth a fortune.

Rule 6: **CELEBRATE** your successes. Find some humor in your failures. Don't take yourself so seriously. Loosen up, and everybody around you will loosen up. Have fun. Show enthusiasm — always. When all else fails, put on a costume and sing a silly song. Then make everybody else sing with you. Don't do a hula on Wall

Street. It's been done. Think up your own stunt. All of this is more important, and more fun, than you think, and it really fools the competition. "Why should we take those cornballs at Wal-Mart seriously?"

Rule 7: LISTEN to everyone in your company. And figure out ways to get them talking. The folks on the front lines — the ones who actually talk to the customer — are the only ones who really know what's going on out there. You'd better find out what they know. This really is what total quality is all about. To push responsibility down in your own organization, and to force good ideas to bubble up within it, you *must* listen to what your associates are trying to tell you.

Rule 8: EXCEED your customers' expectations. If you do, they'll come back over and over. Give them what they want — and a little more. Let them know you appreciate them. Make good on all your mistakes, and don't make excuses — apologize. Stand behind everything you do. The two most important words I ever wrote were on that first Wal-Mart sign: "Satisfaction Guaranteed." They're still up there, and they have made all the difference.

Rule 9: CONTROL your expenses better than your competition. This is where you can always find the competitive advantage. For twenty-five years running — long before Wal-Mart was known as the nation's largest retailer — we ranked number one in our industry for the lowest ratio of expenses to sales. You can make a lot of different mistakes and still recover if you run an efficient operation. Or you can be brilliant and still go out of business if you're too inefficient.

Rule 10: SWIM upstream. Go the other way. Ignore the conventional wisdom. If everybody else is doing it one way, there's a good chance you can find your niche by going in exactly the opposite direction. But be prepared for a lot of folks to wave you down and tell you you're headed the wrong way. I guess in all my years, what I heard more often than anything was: a town of less than 50,000 population cannot support a discount store for very long.

A GUIDE TO "GOLDEN RULE MANAGEMENT"
By Mary Kay Ash, Founder, Mary Kay Cosmetics

1. **Recognize the Value of People.** People are your company's number one asset. When you treat them as you would like to be treated yourself, everyone benefits.

2. **Praise Your People to Success.** Recognition is the most powerful of all motivators. Even criticism can build confidence when it's "sandwiched" between layers of praise.

3. **Tear Down That Ivory Tower.** Keep all doors open. Be accessible to everyone. Remember that every good manager is also a good listener.

4. **Be a Risk-Taker.** Don't be afraid. Encourage your people to take risks, too — and allow room for error.

5. **Be Sales Oriented.** Nothing happens in business until somebody sells something. Be especially sensitive to your customers' needs and desires.

6. **Be a Problem-Solver.** An effective manager knows how to recognize real problems and how to take action to solve them.

7. **Create a Stress-Free Workplace.** By eliminating stress factors — fear of the boss, unreasonable deadlines, and others — you can increase and inspire productivity.

8. **Develop and Promote People From Within.** Upward mobility for employees in your company builds loyalty. People give you their best when they know they'll be rewarded.

9. **Keep Business in Its Proper Place.** At Mary Kay Cosmetics

the order of priorities is faith, family, and career. The real key to success is creating an environment where people are encouraged to balance the many aspects of their lives.

THREE KEYS TO SUCCESS

By S. Truett Cathy, Founder, Chick-fil-A Company

I have learned through more than forty years of business experience these three keys to success that work for all people under every circumstance:

1. You have to *want* to succeed. You have to be willing to make a generous commitment of time and energy. When I went into the restaurant business, I lived next door to the place I called the Dwarf House. When I wasn't on the job, I went back to my room to catch a few hours of sleep. One time I worked thirty-six hours at a stretch without even sitting down.

2. You have to develop *know-how*. Merely putting time and energy into a project isn't enough. You have to study your projected market. You have to develop skills. Prepare yourself physically, mentally and intellectually through formal education.

3. Finally, you have to *do* it. Some people prepare themselves by getting a fine education; they come from a good home; they have the right opportunities, but they blow them because they don't put into action what they have learned.

DAVE'S CHECKLIST FOR GETTING INTO BUSINESS
By R. David Thomas, Founder, Wendy's International

When people ask me how to start a small business, I say, "Go open one up." Then grind it out. Make a profit. No one wants to hear that, but it's true. Nobody's going to tell you anything worth hearing until the customer tells you at the cash register.

Pete Boinis, a good friend of mine and a true innovator in the restaurant industry, has a very sound philosophy about starting a business. He says innovation comes first, but after innovation, two other factors are just as important: motivation and realism. If you don't know how to attract and motivate the best people, it's not likely the business will get off the ground. If the business can only succeed if everything goes one hundred percent as planned, forget it; it won't go anywhere either. You have to have all three ingredients.

Lots of people come to me with ideas for business deals. They want my advice, but most of the time they want my money, too. The first question I always ask is, "What's your plan?" Remember, I didn't have a formal plan. I also wasn't asking anyone to invest in me, either. That's a big difference. If you want investors, you better have a plan you can spell out and it better be convincing. The plan can be exciting and original, but it's even more important that the person behind it be totally committed.

1. **Are you willing to go open one up?** A guy who worked for me opened up a sandwich-and-ice-cream place. He had a possibility. I told him to work at it and make a profit. But, he had a fantasy: He wanted to be big right away. His costs were too high, and he

didn't make any money. Like so many start-ups, he wanted to be a chain overnight. Wendy's made a profit by the sixth week it was in business, but it wasn't a lot of money. Use the first place you open to learn everything you can about how the business works. Most important, will people actually pay money for your product or service?

2. Do you know how your personal plan meshes with your business?

What's your goal? Are you really challenged by this idea, or is it just something to do? What do you want to achieve? How do you feel about working long hours? How much knowledge and experience do you have in the business you are planning to start? How much of your own money do you have on the line?

Are you really ready to do what you want to do? It's all in the timing. Timing includes having all the education, all the on-the-job training, and all the knowledge about that business that you'll need to succeed. And then there is a certain feeling inside that tells you when you are ready. You just know it.

Now, it's O.K. to change your mind. You don't have to have the same plan your whole life, but you have to have a plan. And, at any point in time, you have to be truly serious about that plan.

3. How much will you sacrifice?

A lot of people think they're ready, but they get trapped. They work for a company and can't afford to make changes because their standard of living is too high and they won't give anything up. Sometimes they pay for a big promotion for the rest of their life because they lose control. They have to join country clubs, buy a bigger car and a bigger house. Each thing takes more money. It's not the original cost; it's the upkeep of maintaining the life-style! When a person is ready for a change he has to pick a point and stop. He has to be honest with himself and ask, What do I really want to do and can I do it? Am I willing to put everything I have at risk? How much would I and maybe my family have to give up to make a new start? Does my family understand the risks as well as I do? How will it feel to live in a world without pensions and profit sharing? A world with limited expense accounts and no bonuses? A world without company cars or the status of being with an established company.

The most important thing you'll have to sacrifice is time. You can't start a new business sitting in an armchair. . .You can forget about a vacation, or if you get one, it'll probably last no more than a couple of days. And your family life may well suffer . . . but that can be worked out if they support you and you are committed to supporting them.

4. Do you have enough confidence to succeed?

Sometimes, people are ready and qualified but they haven't got the confidence. Mainly, you look at the experience you have and how successfully you have performed. But you better know what is driving you, too. Give yourself good reasons why you really want to do something and tell yourself that you CAN make it happen.

5. Are you willing to stay small until you really have it right?

If a small businessperson was just starting out in a new concept strategy, the thing that any smart investor or bank will want to know is if you are going to staff small until you get your organization together. It's the "I'm not going to have any overhead." Don't hire people until you can afford them. Once you hire them, you may end up paying them out of your own pocket if the business falters. Or you could lose them as friends or business partners.

6. Are you focused on the right things?

I remember watching the TV show "Moonlighting" with Cybil Shepherd. In it she plays a model — Maddie Hayes — who takes over a detective agency and has gorgeous offices overnight. That's not the way it works when you open a business. The biggest mistake small businesses can make is to build fancy offices. Offices are one of the worst things in the world. But I shouldn't talk. Today we have beautiful offices. Mine overlooks a miniature garden and it has fancy paneling. There are also two handsome chairs by the desk, which Duke University and Ohio State presented to me . . . in honor of the fact, they said, that they could never find a seat in our restaurants. Wise guys.

7. Do you have a good handle on the key expenses?

A first-time operator just launching a business has to be real careful about the amount of money that he sinks into real estate. You can't lock it all up in the location and then have no money to operate with. You need to know all your key costs down to the penny.

8. Do you know about local or national issues that could help or hurt your business?

137

This is a bigger and bigger concern today, but it was big even when we first opened Wendy's. For example, zoning really limited where we could go, and that's what caused all the quick-service restaurants to be clustered in little pockets. Today, you have to figure out what your business does to the environment, or if you'll be able to get qualified workers. There are plenty of traps to steer clear of. A mail-order business better know what will happen to postage rates for the next five years. You have to watch out for issues that don't seem like they are part of your business operations right now because they can have a real impact later on.

9. Do you have your suppliers lined up?

You better have great relationships with your suppliers. Ed Ourant, who is now an executive vice president and one of our top operations people, was a franchisee for several other chains at the time I started Wendy's. He really had connections and helped our people get the right suppliers, and that can be worth gold. You may want to go with cheaper suppliers, but you can pay a big price for that. At first, we had the wrong cups. (We called them "leakers.") We also had some problems in distribution. Ed straightened us out.

10. Are all the legal bases covered?

When a little company starts up, there are always lots of handshake deals everywhere. They say entrepreneurs hate lawyers and I'm an entrepreneur, but if I had one thing to do differently when I opened up Wendy's, it would be to involve lawyers more often. You better get the best legal advice because we live in a legal world, and you need to have the best legal advice you can possible buy.

John Casey, our vice chairman and chief financial officer, is a rare blend of wisdom, common sense, and negotiating skill. John is a lawyer who can put a conflict to bed faster than any manager I know. It was John who taught me that you had to involve lawyers in certain things. You have to protect yourself if people or circumstances don't turn out as you expect. A lawyer can also protect you from your own mistakes. No matter what happens, my advice is simple: Don't get greedy! But don't give your rights away either, and find a lawyer (if you can) who believes both ideas because they are your negotiators if things don't work out. You have to trust them to clean up conflict . . . be sure they have common sense, not just a lot of two-dollar words.

11. Are you ready to deal with the banks?

I sure wasn't when I took over the KFC restaurants in Columbus. One of the first things I wanted to do was to install air-conditioning systems in the four restaurants because I know how air-conditioning could build traffic. But, instead of going downtown to the commercial loan department and talking with somebody who knew something about business, I went to the local branch that did our banking. The loan office there knew about loans for cars and refrigerators but couldn't understand air-conditioning as a business principle. Instead of a loan, what I got was a big lecture on how late these restaurants were in paying their bills and what a lousy risk I was.

My early experiences left me pretty sour on banks and the judgment of bankers. With the savings-and-loan scandal, the junk-bond fiasco, and more banks teetering near the brink of bankruptcy, it's difficult for the businessman to maintain confidence in his bank. That hurts the spirit of entrepreneurship and America's system of free enterprise.

There are many fine people in the banking industry, but some of the bad apples in banking have done plenty of harm. To me, it's a big sin when a bank lends money to people who are poor risks and who aren't likely to pay it back. Every bank should —and the best banks DO — ask the question: "How will you make your payments if things go sour?"

A small businessperson needs a good banker to survive and to expand the company. When you pick a banker, don't go after the one with the fanciest computer system or the slickest brochure. Pick a bank with experience in dealing with small businesses and a banker with a good sense of business judgment.

As for me, I've always tried to do business banking in a very simple way:

■ Pay the bills on time.

■ Put more weight on the cash balance rather than on "cash flow" and other fancy bookkeeping.

■ Learn which banking people you should call on.

■ Always take a clear, sensible business plan with you whenever you ask a bank for money.

■ Pick a bank with a reputation for standing by its customers. (One who won't forget you.)

Does this checklist scare you? It should, and it only lists some of the most important things you have to worry about when you go into business for yourself. I'm the last person to DISCOURAGE anyone from going into business for themselves, but I'm also the FIRST person to encourage people to go into business the right way.

BUSINESS PHILOSOPHY OF WALT DISNEY AND RAY KROC

The story is told that during World War I, Walt Disney and Ray Kroc served in the U. S. Infantry and wound up together in a trench. During a lull in the fighting, they discussed their future goals and plans for when the war was over. During their brainstorming, they decided that they would like to start companies that would have world-wide impact. In doing so, they talked about which common denominators they would choose if they were to limit themselves to three. After much discussion, they narrowed down the list to the following three:

1. Hire the best people you can find for your employees and pay them well.

2. Create for them a learning, creative and expanding work environment.

3. Do all that you can to make them prosper personally.

RECOMMENDED READING LIST

1. *The Holy Bible*

2. *See You at the Top,* Zig Ziglar

3. *The One-Minute Businessman's/Businesswoman's Devotional,* Mike Murdock

4. *Mary Kay on People Management,* Mary Kay Ash

5. *Working Smart,* Dr. Michael LeBoeuf

6. *You and Your Network,* Fred Smith

7. *I Dare You,* William Danforth

8. *Stay in the Game,* Van Crouch

9. *Managing Your Time,* Ted Engstrom and Alec MacKenzie

10. *Lord of the Marketplace,* Myron Rush

11. *Dare to Succeed,* Van Crouch

12. *Life Is Tremendous,* Charlie Jones